Amazon Echo Plus

Advanced User Guide

2017 Updated

By
Steve Wright

Want To STAY Updated with Echo Plus?

Before we begin, I would like to remind you about our **FREE UPDATES** for the latest in Amazon Echo Plus, Alexa and Smart Assistants.

The Amazon Echo Plus and other Alexa Enabled Devices are still in their infancy. In fact you are one of the EARLY ADOPTORS of this technology. The smart assistant industry is changing so fast with new devices, apps and skills being released almost every other day that it is almost impossible to STAY FRESH.

That is where we come in. Staying in the know about new developments in the Smart Assistive Industry is what we are here for. So if you want the LATEST news, tips and tricks we would highly recommend you to please sign up for our FREE newsletter. Do not worry, we hate spam as much as you do and your details will be safe with us.

You can find the link for Signup at the end of this book, in the Conclusion section.

Why You Need this Book

"Alexa, Wake me up at 6 am"

You wake up in the morning at 6 am with the sound of birds chirping. You get up and head straight to your kitchen where a freshly brewed cup of your favourite double espresso is waiting for you. While sipping coffee, Echo Plus reads out the latest news flash and weather report. There is a forecast for rains so you decide to head over to your treadmill instead of going out for a run. In the mean time, your soft-boiled eggs are ready and you have your breakfast while Echo Plus reads out your calendar for the day. Next, you take a quick shower and then ask Echo Plus to order a cab. The cab arrives and you head straight to office.

This is an average morning routine of a regular person, what makes this particular anecdote exceptional is that the all-new Amazon

Echo Plus choreographed this without the touch of a button.

Welcome to your SMART LIFE!

Amazon Echo Plus it the latest Alexa enabled smart speaker by Amazon. It is compatible with an ever-increasing number of smart devices and online platforms. It can answer basic queries, directly control smart devices without a 3rd party Hub, stream music from any of your cloud accounts, receive and make call and much more. It responds to the wake word "Alexa".

Alexa is a cloud-based, voice-activated personal assistant. Unlike Siri or other digital assistants, she has an incredible variety of skills and can be pre-programmed to carry out errands. As you start to use Echo Plus, Alexa adapts to your speech patterns, vocabulary, and personal preferences. And you can also download and install third party Alexa Skills on your Echo Plus device to enhance its capabilities!

This book is written for those who are puzzled by the Amazon Echo Plus. First, are you one who wonders about automation or one who gets things done? Yes, the time for disposing off wires and switches has come. You enter the world of Echo Plus, and Alexa, the wonderful assistant that switches off the lights out when you go to sleep and sends you a message when she senses smoke in the house. Are you ready to be amazed how easier Echo Plus will make your life? Read on and find why the world is going one step smarter with the Amazon Echo Plus.

Alexa combines with countless smart devices and apps to help you automate your daily life. So, let's begin the journey to discover how to use your Amazon Echo Plus to its best advantage.

This book is written from my personal experience and anecdotal evidence from hundreds of fellow Echo Plus Users who have helped me adapt this smart device into my life in the last three years. I am using Amazon Echo Plus and Alexa since the 1st generation Amazon

Echo Plus was released back in 2014. And I published my first Amazon Echo Plus user manual in 2016. In-fact this is my 6th book about Alexa enabled devices.

If you are a tech savvy person, the kind of user that LOVES to figure it out new devices themselves no matter what or is happy to spend a few hours on Google looking for answers then probably you don't need this book.

We are very honest in admitting that you can probably find a lot if the information in this book by looking for it on Amazon Help or Google if you are willing to spend the time and effort to find the information.

But if you were surprised or disappointed to find how little information comes in the box with your all new Amazon Echo Plus and prefer to have at hand, like so many users, a comprehensive, straightforward, step by step Amazon Echo Plus guide, to finding your way around your new device, then this book is definitely for you.

This book will help you save a lot of time and effort of going out and finding all that information to make the best use of your new Amazon Echo Plus. Through this book, our goal is to help you setup Echo Plus and start using it like a pro. After reading this book you will be able to

- Build a Smart Home with Amazon Echo Plus as the Hub.

- Pre-program regular errands like making coffee, reading your calendar and switching off lights at night.

- Shop on Amazon, order pizza and have fun with Easter Eggs.

Learn more, turn up the thermostat, open the shades and put on your favorite music...hmm "Alexa, turn the thermostat up..."

Table of Contents

Introduction

Welcome! Thank You for buying this book. We are excited to have you Onboard our journey to the world of Amazon Echo Plus and Alexa. Before we begin let me remind you to Signup for our Alexa Newsletter so that you remain updated with all the latest developments with Amazon Echo Plus. The Signup information is available at the end if this book in the Conclusion.

How To Use This Book

Feel free to dip in and out of different chapters, but we would suggest reading the whole book from start to finish to get a clear overview of all the information contained in this book. We have purposely kept this book short, sweet and to the point so that you can consume it in an hour and get straight on with enjoying your

Amazon Echo Plus.

In a nutshell Amazon Echo Plus is a voice-activated speaker from Amazon that

- Acts as your smart personal assistant
- Performs digital errands at your command
- Connects and controls all of your smart devices
- Acts as your Smart Home Hub

Essentially Amazon Echo Plus is a speaker and it functions like a personal assistant. Amazon launched the 1st Generation Amazon Echo in 2014 and it was the first major product that was launched by this company after Kindle. Amazon has sold hundreds of Amazon Echo and other Alexa enabled devices and started the trend of Smart Voice Controlled Home Assistants.

Amazon has just released Amazon Echo Plus, an updated version of its wildly popular Amazon Echo, featuring inbuilt Smart Home Hub, a fresh look and better audio. The Amazon Echo Plus is priced at $149.99 and can be ordered from the Amazon website.

The New Smart Home Hub

Many simply assume that the Amazon Echo Plus is a regular speaker. However, calling Echo Plus a speaker is far from accurate. It definitely does function as an excellent speaker, but it is primarily a personal assistant that can help you with

- Running your daily chores and errands at Home and Office
- Freeing up you time by carrying out repetitive tasks
- Calling or messaging anyone with a supported Echo Plus device or the Alexa App on their phone for FREE.
- Controlling your smart devices – Lights, Thermostat, Crockpot etc
- Informing you about News, Sports Updates, Weather, Traffic and more
- Playing your favorite music at a voice command

And much more....

The Echo Plus has been designed to respond to voice commands. It will reply if you call its "Wake Word". You can choose from among four of the following wake words.

- Alexa
- Echo Plus
- Amazon
- Computer

When you want your Echo Plus to do something, then you will have to start out by saying the Wake Word. The device will acknowledge the same and you don't even need a remote or your phone for turning it on. This does sound good, doesn't it?

You must definitely be curious to learn more about this device. It is so much more than a personal assistant and performs more functions than Siri and Cortana can. The Echo Plus can be compared to the efficient JARVIS that helps Iron Man with his work.

The All New Amazon Echo Plus brings a new dimension of supplementary ease to a smart home. Users can control settings of interconnected devices through a simple voice command. By doing away with dials, switches, and buttons, Echo Plus helps multiple users with different accents activate or change settings on digital devices from far away. It is especially useful for people with disability.

You can 'command' your Echo Plus with voice messages that last for 2 minutes at a time. You would know soon how amazing it feels to have an assistant that does exactly as told and gets smarter with every interaction.

What is Alexa?

While Amazon Echo Plus is just a speaker, Alexa is the all powerful cloud based voice control system that enables hands free control of your home, devices and appliances. You can speak to your Alexa Device i.e. Echo Plus and get all your commands fulfilled. Open the Door, Switch on the Light or Play Music. What more, as you interact with Alexa, it keeps on getting smarter and faster. Alexa also comes with a variety of skills, as you will see later. These skills are like apps in your smartphone. They carry out specific tasks and helps enhance the use of your Echo Plus.

Interestingly, Alexa gets its name from the library of Alexandria. It was one of the biggest and the most significant libraries in ancient world.

Features That Make Echo Plus Amazing

Inbuilt Smart Home Hub

The Echo Plus comes with an inbuilt Zigbee smart home hub. This is the outstanding feature of Echo Plus that none of the alexa-enabled devices have. Unlike other Echo devices that need an external smart home hub to communicate with smart home devices, the Echo Plus can directly control them through voice commands or pre programmed routines. So this makes setting up a smart home lot easier. No more buying a smart home hub or using multiple apps to control all your smart devices.

However, please remember that there are still certain smart devices that need a 3rd party smart home Hub. So if you already have a Smart Home setup, please do checkout if all your devices can be controlled using Echo Plus.

Ease of use

The Amazon Echo Plus is extremely easy to use. In fact, it is easier than using a cell phone. You don't have to worry about inserting a SIM card, installing apps, registering your name or any such things. You will simply have to turn the device on for using it.

Even if you have never made use of personal assistant service, it doesn't take more than a few hours to get a hang of it. The step-by-step instructions in this book will help you in getting started. Using an Echo Plus is pretty easy. You will simply have to plug it in, follow the simple instructions, and that's about it.

Built

The Amazon Echo Plus is a beautiful device. It is one of the best looking speakers available in the market. It comes into three styles to fit into your home's décor. Because of its size, you can choose to place the device on a tabletop or it can be easily concealed if you wish to. The classy and sleek look of this device makes it really attractive.

The LED lights change colors according to the commands that the device receives. When the Echo is processing a command, the lights turn BLUE.

The four buttons on top of the Echo Plus are POWER, MUTE,

VOLUME UP and VOLUME DOWN. The Power button is for switching Echo Off and the Mute button prevents the Echo from listening to your conversations. Amazon has done away with the volume ring on the 1st generation Amazon Echo and replaced it with volume up and down buttons.

Lighting

The way the Echo Plus changes colors, tells you what's happening with the device. When the Echo Plus is switching on, the light will turn WHITE and it will have a CYAN RING around it. When it turns ORANGE, this means that the device is connecting to the Internet or the WiFi network. The light will turn a darker shade of orange if it connects to the network and if not, it will turn VOILET. If this happens, try turning off the WiFi and then turning it back on for connecting your device. When you are changing the volume of the Echo Plus, it will show a white ring. This ring turns RED when you mute the Echo Plus.

Privacy

This seems to be a huge concern for a lot of people who make use of personal assistant devices like the Echo Plus. Echo Plus is designed to pick up every word that it hears and it makes use of its cloud processing system. In such a case, how will you make sure that your personal information isn't being divulged?

You needn't worry about this at all. When you are discussing any private matters, you can just mute the device by pressing the MUTE button on top of the Echo Plus. Press this switch, and the Echo Plus will stop collecting any information.

Sound

The all-new Amazon Echo Plus has got an amazing sound quality. It is powered by Dolby audio processing and produces incredibly clear audio with crisp vocals and dynamic bass. One of the primary functions Echo Plus was designed for is playing music and it, therefore, comes with a good woofer system. The 2.5-inch woofers can produce remarkable sound and the 0.8-inch tweeter that it has picks up on bass and enhances its sound quality as well.

These two parts are placed in a sequence inside the Echo Plus. You can simply ask the Echo Plus to play your playlist or a particular song and it'll do so. The sound quality of Echo Plus's speaker is wonderful. It has a 360-degree surround sound system. This enables the device to fill the surroundings with music. It has got a clear speaking voice and you can understand what it says easily, even in noisy surroundings. Children find it easy to understand the Echo Plus and it is quite an entertaining playmate for them since it responds like a human being.

Voice recognition

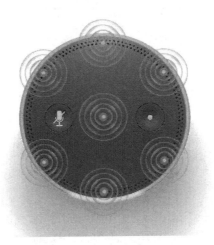

The all-new Amazon Echo Plus is equipped with 2nd generation far-field technology. The Echo Plus can understand you easily since it is a voice-activated device. It is incredibly important that it understands you individually and can recognize the voices of different users.

The high-tech audio sensors and the processing system for natural voice enable it to hear any kind of voice, high or low pitch, male or female irrespective of their age. The sensors make Echo Plus a very sensitive device. Since these sensors are positioned all over the body it is extremely easy for the device to pick up signals from anywhere in the room even in noisy environment.

There are seven sensors placed on its outer body and they are placed equidistantly. These top quality sensors are extremely efficient. The voice canceling system will enable the Echo Plus to listen to your instructions even over loud music. Usually, you won't have to speak loudly for the Echo Plus to process your command as it is designed to pick up your voice among all the noise at home and in the office. And Echo Plus is always listening for your commands.

I would like to add here that some people have experienced Echo Plus going deaf in presence of LOUD MUSIC. This issue has been reported to Amazon and they are working to rectify it. In the meantime one quick hack is to use the REMOTE when playing loud music. The remote can be bought separately here.

Expandability

The Echo Plus keeps getting upgraded and new features are being added to it all the time. You don't have to buy a new device to activate all these new features. Amazon gives automatic access to all the Echo Plus users to make the most of these updates. With constant innovation, the benefits offered by it are also increasing.

You can dim your lights or regulate the room temperature with just one command. Echo Plus is an impressive device and with regular updates new features are added to this smart device.

Which Alexa Device is Best Suited for You?

Amazon offers a number of Alexa Enabled devices-

- Amazon Echo

- Amazon Echo Plus

- Amazon Echo Plus

9

- Amazon Echo Tap

- Amazon Echo Look

- Amazon Echo Show

- Amazon Echo Spot

The difference between these devices is that each one is best suited to a particular lifestyle, be at home, on the go, being your personal stylist, facilitating video calling, or as an enhancement to your current audio setup.

All New Amazon Echo

Get this one if you only require one device in your home and want to experience the fullness of Echo's sound quality from a central place in your house.

Echo is Amazon's flagship Alexa device, and will give you the fullest experience.

It's a 14.8 cm tall cylinder that has full support for voice commands and Alexa functionality. So you can command Echo with the wake word 'Alexa', and it will respond.

Technical Specifications

- Weight: 821 grams
- Price: $99.99 – $119.99
- Size: 148mm x 88mm x 88mm
- Colors: Charcoal Fabric, Heather Gray Fabric, Sandstone Fabric, Walnut Finish, Oak Finish, Silver Finish
- Audio: 2.5" woofer 0.6" tweeter (360-degree)
- Connectivity: Dual-band, dual-antenna Wi-Fi (MIMO) 802.11a/b/g/n support

Power: Wall adapter with 1.8m cable

Amazon Echo Plus

Get this one if you only require one device in your home and also want Alexa to control all your smart home devices directly without the interference of any external smart home hub.

It's a 14.8 cm tall cylinder that has full support for voice commands and Alexa functionality. So you can command Echo with the wake word 'Alexa', and it will respond.

- Weight: 954 grams

- Price: $149.99
- Size: 235mm x 84mm x 84mm
- Colors: Black, White, Silver
- Audio: 2.5" woofer 0.8" tweeter (360-degree)
- Connectivity: Dual-band, dual-antenna Wi-Fi (MIMO) 802.11a/b/g/n support

Amazon Echo Plus

Best suited if you have a big house with multiple rooms or have an amazing sound system already in place. Either way, single or multiple Dot devices can be plugged in and you can access Alexa on your surround system from anywhere in your house.

Specifications:

- Weight: 163 grams
- Price: $49.99
- Size: 83.5 x 83.5 x 32mm
- Colors: White, Black
- Audio: Built-in speaker, 3.5mm stereo output

- Connectivity: Dual-band Wi-Fi 802.11/a/b/g/n, Bluetooth connectivity
- Power: Power adapter 9W, USB charging cable

Dot is the smallest of the Alexa speakers. It's has full Alexa functionality, but has only one single, tiny speaker for Alexa voice feedback. So instead of using it as your primary speaker you can link it up to your existing sound system, either via a Bluetooth or 3.5mm jack, to get a more Echo-like experience.

Amazon TAP

If you need assistance on the go Amazon Tap is your best bet, it also doubles up as your Bluetooth speaker.

Specifications:

- Weight: Tap – 470 grams | Dock – 109 grams
- Price: $129.99
- Size: Tap – 159 x 66 x 66mm | Dock – 15 x 66 x 66mm
- Colors: Black

- Audio: Dual 1.5-inch drivers and dual passive radiators for bass extension
- Connectivity: Single Band Wi-Fi 802.11b/g/n Bluetooth
- Power: Charging dock (9 hours of music playback)

Amazon Tap is for people who need Alexa on the go. This portable speaker has full Alexa functionality but the speaker quality is not as good as Echo. Another key difference is that, unlike Echo or DOT, Amazon Tap is NOT always on. You need to press a button to activate Alexa, rather than using a wake word. Tap is wireless, and at full charge you can get up to 9 hours of continuous playback.

Amazon Echo Show

The Echo Show offers everything you love about Alexa, in addition to the new video and touchscreen controls. It is a dedicated, hands-free video calling command center.

Specifications:

- Weight: 1170 grams
- Price: $229.99
- Size: 187mm x 187mm x 90mm
- Colors: Black / White
- Audio: Dual 2 inch stereo speakers
- Connectivity: Dual Band Wi-Fi 802.11b/g/n Bluetooth
- Power: Power adapter, 6 ft. USB charging cable
- Camera: 5MP

Amazon Show is for smart families. It lets you make hands free video calls to friends and family, keep a check on the front door or monitor your baby's room. You can now watch video briefings, Amazon Video content, see music lyrics, photos, weather forecasts, to-do and shopping lists all hands free - Just Ask.

Amazon Echo Look

Amazon Look is your cloud based fashion consultant. Using a hands free camera and machine learning guided by fashion experts it can give you recommendations on what to wear. Presently you can purchase it by invitation only. Request for an invitation here.

Specifications:

- Price: $199.99 or £156
- Size: Look – 6.3" x 2.4"x 2.4"
- Colors: Black / White
- Camera: 5MP camera and Intel RealSense SR300 for depth-sensing technology
- Speaker: 1.6 watt speaker
- Processor: Intel Atom x5-Z8350 processor for advanced technology and processing capabilities

Amazon Look can use voice commands to take photos or videos of you and be your style assistant .In addition the device comes with all the other features of Alexa, such as the ability to read the news, set alarms, get traffic and weather updates, control smart home devices and play music.

Setup Your Echo Plus

What's in the Box

- Amazon Echo Plus
- Power Adapter
- Micro USB cable
- 1 Page Quick Start Guide

Once you open the box, you will see the main unit. Echo Plus is a small cylindrical device 9.3 inches tall and it will take about 4 sq. inches of space on your tabletop. It has got speaker holes on its sides and on its top. It has got voice sensors, speakers and lights.

The cylindrical shape that it comes in helps in minimizing the space it requires. However, it is more effective if there's a little room around the device for better reception. The subwoofer system is present in the perforated base so be careful while handling it. The light ring on top of the Echo Plus turns blue when the device is switched on.

It is powered with the help of a plug-in adapter. You can put it on a metallic surface or even stick it against your cabinet depending on your convenience.

Don't let the size of the Echo Plus fool you, it is extremely useful and worth the price. Its size allows you to place it anywhere and it is powerful enough to pick up on sounds, making it effective.

3 Step Setup Instructions

Simple to Set Up & Use

1. Plug in Echo

2. Connect to the internet with the Alexa App

3. Just ask for music, weather, news, and more

Alexa App is available for Android, iOS, and Fire devices.

Step #1: Install your Amazon Echo Plus in A Safe Place

First, decide where you're going to keep your Echo Plus. A table is probably best for ease of access, but it shouldn't be the dining table – there's too much risk of damage from spills or jostling. Try to find a place near the center of the house so that the sound can travel throughout.

Place the Echo Plus directly on the table surface. Don't cushion it with Styrofoam or the like, as this tends to degrade sound quality with reverberations.

Try to find a place at least 10 inches from the walls, windows or any obstructions.

- Connect the micro-USB cable into the micro-USB port of your Echo Plus.
- Plug the other end of your micro-USB cable into the 9W adaptor supplied and then plug it into a power supply.
- The LED light ring on top of your Echo Plus will turn blue and will begin to spin. In a minute, the color will change to Orange and Alexa will greet you.

Step #2: Setup your Echo Plus using Alexa App

Downloading the Alexa App

Now, go to the store on your mobile or computer. This could be Google Play Store, Apple App Store or Amazon Appstore. Instead, you can type *alexa.amazon.com* in your browser search bar. Search and download the *Alexa app* for Fire OS, Android or iOS. Sign into your account and follow the instructions in the app/website to complete the setup.

(Please note that Alexa app is not supported on Kindle Fire 1st or 2nd Generations)

Connect Your Echo Plus to Wifi

Be sure to connect dual-band Wi-Fi networks and not use mobile hotspots. It will not work when you use ad-hoc networks that are connected peer-to-peer.

- Open the Alexa app and go to **Settings**.
- Select your device and click on **Update Wi-Fi**.
- For first time users, click on **Select a new device**.
- Now, press the *Action* button on the Echo Plus device.
- The light will turn orange and you will see a list of networks appear on your mobile device. Select your Wi-Fi network and type the password if required.
- For cases where your network is not visible, scroll down the list and select **Add a Network**.
- If this does not work, click on **Rescan**.

- Now click **Connect** and Alexa is ready for use.

Step #3: Talk to Your Amazon Echo Plus for the First Time

To begin, we use the wake word – *Alexa*. *'Alexa, play me some music'*. Or *'Alexa, what is the weather like today?'* When your voice reaches Echo Plus, the circular, blue LED lights on top of Echo Plus lights up – she is listening, and once your command is analyzed, Alexa will reply.

Alexa listens every second for her 'wake' word through her seven microphones. This way you do not have to raise your voice and can call her over the din of conversation or music. If many people ask her questions, Alexa picks out the individual accents of the people and separates the questions with ease. Then, you get the answers. *"Music playing"* and *"The weather is sunny with day temperatures of 90 degrees."*

Voice Training Your Echo Plus

Now that the setup is complete its time for fun!

Say hello to your new Personal Assistant. Its this chapter we will learn about all the errands you can get your new Echo Plus to run for you and start easing your life immediately. With the help of a voice command you will get the latest in sports, weather and traffic and news, order a cab or listen to your favorite Audiobook. But first let's train Echo to recognize and understand our Voice.

Voice Training

It's important to train your Echo Plus if you want it to perform well. It's a fairly simple process, so let's get started.

It's best to get all members of your family to take turns speaking to Echo Plus. Before we start commanding our new Voice Assistant, we need to introduce everyone in the house to Echo Plus. So line up everyone who would be using the Echo Plus and make them speak to it, one after the other. This is a really important step of the setup process and is referred to as VOICE TRAINING.

Doing this will help your Echo Plus respond accordingly and it does get better with practice. Eventually, it will be able to identify different users through their voice and use their name while responding to them.

Each user should go through voice training multiple times. It will also help the users get accustomed to the way Echo Plus responds to your queries.

For starting a voice training session, you will have to open the Alexa app. Then go to the navigation panel on the home page, and pick the Voice Training option. Press the Start button.

The next step is for you to say a phrase for the Echo Plus to listen to and comprehend. Try to include complex words to ensure that the Echo Plus can understand them. When you finish a phrase, choose the Next option at the bottom of the app screen to move on to another one.

Speak in a natural voice, even if you have a heavy accent. You don't have to be too close to the device; it should be able to accept commands from any part of the room.

Once you're done speaking, you should introduce the next member of your family to the Echo Plus. They can then do the same as you just did – speak phrases so that the Echo Plus can listen to them and train it.

Each of you should speak about 25 phrases, trying to incorporate as many words as possible. The more the Echo Plus hears, the more it understands.

You can press the Pause button at any time, and if you think you've made a mistake then you can pick the Cancel option. Then press Repeat to try again.

Once everyone is done and you have recorded all the phrases, you can press the End Session button.

Your Echo Plus will now be able to understand you better. It should take most commands with ease and will rarely get confused. However, you can't expect it to be perfect. The Echo's voice recognition is very good, but a perfect voice recognition technology has yet to be developed, and it will make the occasional mistake.

Once the Echo Plus is familiar with everyone, it will remember the preferences of every individual. The way it responds would be more relevant and it can make suggestions based on the user activity. For instance, if anyone in your household keeps asking for news updates, then the next time that user calls out to the Echo Plus; it will start reading out the news updates automatically.

Fortunately, learning is an ongoing process with the Amazon Echo Plus. It will learn new things constantly and better itself with time. You will be pleasantly surprised at the amount of improvement the Echo Plus demonstrates over several months as it trains itself to suit your needs.

Please remember, Echo Plus can identify up to a maximum of 20 voices, as long as they aren't similar. And, Echo Plus will NOT respond to someone whose voice it doesn't recognize. It will not take any commands from a stranger even if they turn it off and then switch it on again. A user needs to be introduced to Echo Plus before it can recognize a new voice.

Alexa Commands

You can make these commands work on all Alexa enabled devices. Just use the following commands.

- *"Alexa, Stop"*
- *"Alexa, Volume [number Zero to Ten]"*
- *"Alexa, Unmute"*
- *"Alexa, Mute"*
- *"Alexa, Repeat"*
- *"Alexa, Cancel"*
- *"Alexa, Louder"*
- *"Alexa, Volume Up"*
- *"Alexa, Volume Down"*
- *"Alexa, Turn Down"*
- *"Alexa, Turn Up"*
- *"Alexa, Help"*

How to Get Help from Alexa

When you've got a question about your Echo Plus, you can simply ask Alexa about it.

To get some help from Alexa, just say the **Alexa** word followed by the following questions:

- *"What can you do?"*
- *"What are your new features?"*
- *"What do you know?"*
- *"Can you do math?"*
- *"How can/do I play music?"*
- *"How can/do I add music?"*
- *"What is Prime Music?"*
- *"What is Audible?"*
- *"What is Connected Home?"*
- *"What is Voice Cast?"*
- *"How can/do I pair to Bluetooth?"*
- *"How can/do I connect my calendar?"*
- *"What is an Alexa skill?"*
- *"How can/do I use skills?"*
- *"How can/do I set an alarm?"*

How to Ask Alexa for Basic Calculations

If you manage accounts or have to deal with figures, having a voice-activated calculator is quite helpful. The Echo can help you with simple calculations and even the more complicated ones. You can get it to perform such functions without having to touch the keypad.

- *"Alexa, one thousand eight hundred seventy six (1,876) divided by four"*
- *"Alexa, three point four eight six (3.486) times twenty four"*
- *"Alexa, convert 12 feet to centimeters"*
- *"Alexa, convert 7 tablespoons to milliliters"*

- *"Alexa, convert 35 Fahrenheit to Celsius"*
- *"Alexa, how many miles are in thirty kilometers?"*

How to Ask Alexa for Cooking Conversions

- *"Alexa, how many teaspoons in two tablespoon?"*
- *"Alexa, how many tablespoons in eighteen teaspoons?"*
- *"Alexa, how many pints in four gallons?"*
- *"Alexa, how many cups in four quarts?"*

Getting Information from Echo Plus

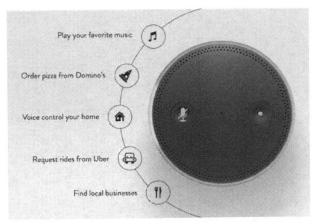

The next thing would be to customize your Echo Plus. You should add your LOCATION. This enables Echo Plus to serve you better. If it isn't able to identify your location, then you can enter your zip code and try. You can also select the date format and the option of using metric system is up to you as well. Cloud computing will be set up automatically and you don't have to do anything else. The last step would be to select a Wake Name. Alexa is the default name. However, you can choose Echo, Amazon or Computer as well.

Let me add here that limited choice of Wake Words is a big issue with consumers who want a more personalized device. Amazon is working to rectify this issue. But as of now we just have to work with these 4 wake words until they allow us to use our own customized wake words.

How to get Localized Information

- Go to Settings in the Alexa App
- Tap on Echo Plus Device Location
- Enter your Address with Zip Code
- Tap Save Changes

This will get you weather reports, local news and even pre-recorded shows relative to your area.

Ask Echo Plus for Latest Weather Report

To get the latest weather reports from your area use the following commands:

- *"Alexa, what's the weather?"*
- *"Alexa, will it rain tomorrow?"*
- *"Alexa, what's the weather in Los Angeles this weekend?"*
- *"Alexa, what's the weather in Dallas?"*
- *"Alexa, what will the weather be like in Boston tomorrow?"*
- *"Alexa, what's the weather in Silver City, New Mexico?"*
- *"Alexa, what's the extended forecast for Chicago?"*
- *"Alexa, what will the weather be like in San Diego on Thursday?"*
- *"Alexa, is it going to snow on Monday?"*

Setup Alarms and Timers on Your Echo Plus

For Alarms use the following commands

- *"Wake me up at [time]."*
- *"Set an alarm for [time]."*
- *"Set an alarm for [amount of time] from now."*

For Countdown Timers use the following commands

- *"Set a timer for [amount of time]."*
- *"Set the timer for [time]."*

For a comprehensive list of all the alarm and timer commands and the change the alarm sound volume please refer to <u>this</u> page on the Amazon Help.

Ask Echo Plus for the Latest Flash Briefings

How to Hear Flash Briefings

You don't need a newspaper to keep up with current events anymore – and with the Echo Plus, you don't even have to look at a monitor or tablet. All you have to do is ask it for your flash briefing and it will read out all the news bulletins for you. It will give you at least the headlines, and might also read a snippet of the accompanying articles.

To hear flash briefings of the latest new updates, you can configure your Alexa App to include news from various sources: BBC, Economist, TMZ, and NPR etc. To hear the news, just say *"Alexa, what's my Flash Briefing?"* and Echo Plus will play the news from your selected sources.

Configuring Flash Briefings

- Open the Alexa app
- Tap the left navigation panel,
- Go to Settings
- Select **Flash Briefing**
- Customize your Flash Briefing: Shows, News Headlines, Weather Updates etc.

Ask Echo Plus for Real-time Traffic Updates

Traffic is a big headache for most commuters, but the Echo Plus can now help you beat it. You have to use the Alexa app to add in your origin and destination points, but after that, you can just ask the Echo Plus what traffic looks like between them. It will let you know the shortest route, as well as the best route in terms of current traffic conditions.

How to Configure the Traffic Information

To get the most efficient routes from your Echo Plus

- Go to settings on your Alexa App
- Tap on Change Address
- Input the address in the FROM and TO fields
- Tap Save Changes

This will get you the most accurate traffic information for your desired route

Get the Latest Sports Scores

The Echo Plus can also give you sports news, of course, but it goes one better than that by providing live scores as well. Gone are the days of repeatedly clicking the refresh button on a web page to keep track of a game. It currently works with the NBA, NFL, NHL, WNBA, MLB and a few other major leagues. Tennis and mixed martial arts haven't been added to this list as of now.

Just ask

- *"Alexa, what the score (team name) game?"*
- *"Alexa, when does (team name) play?"*

Order UBER with a Voice Command

- Open the Alexa App and tap the three bar menu on Top Left Corner
- Tap Skills
- Under Skills, search for Uber
- Enable the Uber Skill
- Sign In to your Uber Account and tap Allow

For office-goers who use Uber often, pulling out the phone to call up Uber may become tedious. So, commanding Alexa seems to be more attractive. *"Alexa, Ask Uber for a ride."* And Alexa comes back with, *"Your Uber ride is on its way."* You understand the charm Echo has. One likes to talk to Alexa rather than a cab driver or manager anytime!

Get Echo Plus to Read Your Kindle Books

- *"Alexa, Read my Kindle book"*
- *"Alexa, Read my book <title>"*
- *"Alexa, Play the Kindle book <title>"*
- *"Alexa, Read < title>"*

Listen to Your Audio Books

- *"Alexa, Read <title>"*
- *"Alexa, Play the book <title>"*
- *"Alexa, Play the audiobook <title>"*
- *"Alexa, Play <title> from Audible"*

Get Echo Plus to Read Your Calendar

How to Connect your Google Calendar to Alexa

You can pair your Google Calendar with your Echo Plus, which makes it easy to keep your whole schedule in one place and access it whenever you need to. You'll be more efficient at home and in the office, and you'll never have to miss another deadline or event. You can activate this feature by going to Settings in the Alexa app.

Though you can use any calendar you like, the Google Calendar will help you take the first step.

To connect follow these simple steps:

- Open the Alexa App in your mobile
- Click on *Settings > Calendar > Link Google Calendar Account*

You log in with your Google account and when you activate Alexa, you can check your schedule though you cannot write in new events. For that, you need to integrate the IFTTT recipe Add Amazon Echo To-Do to Google Calendar.

There are other recipes as well that can come handy, such as Add your To Do list to Google Calendar or Add a Sports Game to your Google Calendar. To check the complete list please visit IFTTT.COM

Do this on your calendar

"Alexa, what's on my calendar?" or *"Alexa, when is my next event?"* will give you the answers, *"You have a golf game with Martin at 3:00 PM today"* and *"Your next event is at 11:00 AM – A get together with your stockholders."*

When naming your tasks, you must take care to see you avoid the use of the first person. *"I'm home"* or *"I want the news"* will not be as Alexa-friendly as *"Arrive Home"* and *"News Update."*

Add a household member to your Amazon Echo Plus

You can add multiple household members to your Echo Plus. You can share digital content with other members and also collaborate with them on the to-do lists, calendars etc.

- Open the Alexa app
- Go to Settings
- Go to Household Profile
- Sign in to your account.
- Click Continue.
- Enter the amazon account information for the person you want to add.
- Click Join Household.

If you want to check which member profile is active use the following commands

- "Alexa, which account is this?"
- "Alexa, which profile am I using?"

Please remember that once other members are on Echo Plus they will be able to shop from your account as well. For an additional

Remove a household member from Amazon Echo Plus

- Go to Settings.
- Go to In an Amazon household with [user name] and tap
- Tap Remove User

Play Your Favorite Music On Echo Plus

Echo Plus can also access your Amazon digital music store. This means that you will be able to select what you want from a wide range of artists and genres. It will keep a track of what you like listening to and will provide you similar suggestions. Not just this, but it can also respond to your requests really quickly.

Playing Music on Echo Plus is the biggest activity reported by Amazon Echo Plus owners. Usually, we don't have a hand free for changing the song on your stereo or iPod. With an Echo, you don't have to worry about changing a song manually. You can tell Echo Plus to play the song or the playlist that you want to listen, and it will. You can create multiple playlists on Echo Plus. It is programmed to automatically play your favorite song based on the number of times it has been played. The smart voice recognition system will enable the device to recognize the speaker and play the song that that person likes. Echo Plus can also be directed to buy music from the Amazon store.

Alexa supports a growing number of free and subscription-based

streaming services on Amazon devices

- Amazon Music
- Prime Music
- Spotify Premium
- Pandora
- TuneIn
- iHeartRadio
- Audible

Music Commands

Basic

Say the **Alexa** word followed by any of the following commands.

- *"Play"*
- *"Skip"*
- *"Skip back"*
- *"Pause"*
- *"Continue"*
- *"Next"*
- *"Previous"*
- *"Repeat"*
- *"Shuffle"*
- *"Loop"*
- *"Volume 4"*
- *"Softer"*
- *Turn it Up"*

Equalizer Commands to Change Bass, Midrange and Treble

- "Alexa, turn up the bass"

- "Alexa, increase the midrange"
- "Alexa, turn down the treble"

Advanced

Say the **Alexa** word followed by any of the following commands.

- *"Play some music"*
- *"Play the song, [title]"*
- *"Play the album, [title]"*
- *"Play songs by [artist]"*
- *"Play some [genre] music"*
- *"Play some [genre name] music from Prime"*
- *"Listen to my [title] playlist"*
- *"Shuffle my [title] playlist"*

These commands will work with the following services

- Amazon Music
- Audible
- Prime Music

But some commands will vary with third party music streaming services like Spotify and TuneIn. Please refer to this exhaustive list of commands for playing music from different services.

Music Hacks

These are some of the top IFTTT applets for Echo music lovers. Some quick hacks you can execute.

Keep a Google Spreadsheet of Songs you Listen on Echo
Trigger Music on Your Phone
Dim Lights when you play music on Echo
Play a Song when a Timer is Finished

How to Migrate Your Music Files to Amazon

Your Amazon Echo device cannot playback any audio files that are stored in your Amazon Cloud Drive. However, the Echo can play files that are stored in your Amazon Music Library or Audible library, in case of audiobooks you own.

I am pleased to tell you that each Amazon customer has an account for Amazon Music Library. It does not matter whether you have signed up for premium version, you will have an account. If you look at the picture below, the link for you amazon drive is right there.

You can store up to 250 songs on your Music Library in Amazon for free. But, Amazon Prime members get unlimited access to the Amazon Prime Music Library. They are able to upload files from their Amazon Prime Music Library to their personal music libraries. The best part is that these files or the music you purchase online from Amazon does not count towards the 250-song free upload limit.

What if I have got a Large Playlist?

If you have got a huge, *personal* music library outside Amazon, it offers a premium subscription as well. For $24.99/year, you will be able to upload, play and store a max of 250,000 tracks. And the song purchases you make from Amazon do not count towards this 250,000 tracks limit.

What if I don't want to migrate my Music to Amazon?

If you are like me and you don't want to go through the hassle of migrating your whole playlist to Amazon Music Player, I understand that totally. I have another solution for you. With Bluetooth, Alexa connects directly to either iTunes or Google Music. You can pair Alexa to any device with Bluetooth using the following command.

- *"Alexa, Pair"*

Make sure your device is within the range for Echo Plus. Once Alexa detects your device it will instruct you to go to it and select Echo from the Bluetooth pairing screen. Once the device is paired, open the app you normally use for iTunes / Google Music playback and start some music.

The commands you can use with Alexa for Bluetooth playback control:

- *"Alexa, Play"*
- *"Alexa, Pause"*
- *"Alexa, Restart"*
- *"Alexa, Resume"*
- *"Alexa, Stop"*
- *"Alexa, Previous"*
- *"Alexa, Next"*

You can pair multiple devices with Echo Plus.

Multi-Room Music with Echo Devices

Suppose you have multiple Echo devices all over your house and want to play the same music/radio on all of them simultaneously. That is now possible without any 3rd party integration. To do that, you need to make a smart home group of Echo devices.

The services that you can use for the multi room music feature are:
- Amazon Music
- TuneIn
- iHeartRadio
- Pandora

Spotify and Sirius will be included soon.

To create a smart home group, follow these steps:

- Open Alexa App
- Go to the **Menu**
- Select **Smart Home**
- Select **Groups**
- Select **Add Group**
- Select the group type:
  - **Multi-Room Music Group**: Stream the same music station, song, or playlist to compatible devices.
- Enter a **name** for the group you created.

- Select the smart devices you want to add to the group
- Select **Save**

Bingo! Now, whenever you want to use multi-room playback just say the following command:

- "Alexa, turn on (group name)"

And your music will come live.

Connect with other Music Devices and Apps

Choose from the many devices to add quality to your music scene. iHeartRadio, TuneIn, Pandora and Spotify Premium top this list of must haves. And for those who have no subscriptions as yet to these channels, there is Amazon Music Library from where you can stream Prime Music.

How to Use Spotify on Echo Plus?

Spotify is one of the top apps that amazing integration with Echo Plus.

Setup

- Open the Alexa app
- Tap the Menu button
- Go to Music & Books

- Tap Spotify
- Tap Link account
- Log into Spotify
- Tap OKAY

Make Spotify your Default Music Player

- Open Alexa app
- Go to Settings,
- Tap customize my music service preferences
- Under My preferred music source, select Spotify.
- Tap Done

Spotify Hacks

Add Songs Played by Echo to Spotify Playlist
Add Alexa Music to Spotify
Every time a song is Played on Prime Music add it to a Spotify Playlist
Add Songs from YouTube videos You like to Spotify Playlist

How to Use Pandora on Echo Plus?

- Tap on Alexa app
- Tap Menu in top left corner
- Open Music and Book and Tap Pandora in the sub menu.
- On the registration page for Pandora, tap *"Link account"*
- If you have a Pandora account Sign IN if not then Sign UP.

Once the setup process is completed, your station list will be seen on your Alexa app.

iHeartRadio

This radio station has a wide range of genres ranging from Hip Hop and R&B, Top 40 & Pop, Classic Rock, Oldies, Jazz and much more.

TuneIn

TuneIn likewise has many genres though the crowd here is younger.

You can also use TuneIn to listen to your favorite Podcasts.

- *"Alexa, Play [number on the dial] [station name] on TuneIn"*
- *"Alexa, play [podcast name] on TuneIn"*

How to Access Another Household Member's Music Library On Your Echo Plus

To achieve this, set up *Amazon Household Profiles* in your Alexa app. This will give access of your Amazon account to the second person and also will allow that person to make purchases, both physical and digital, on your account using voice commands to the Echo Plus.

You can prevent undesired purchases by adding a password. To setup the password,

- Go to the Voice Purchasing inside the Amazon Household Profile
- Enter a 4-digit confirmation code that users will speak at the time of purchases to confirm their identity.

After the Household Profile setup, you are able to switch accounts on you Echo and access all the content by using the following command

- *"Alexa, switch accounts"*

How to check whose profile is in use currently

- *"Alexa, which account is this?"*

Voice Calling and Messaging

Alexa's new Calling & Messaging feature lets you make calls, send messages and even leave a voice message between any two Echo devices . The service is free and works regardless of the distance between the two devices .The highlights of this new feature are Skype like conferencing and automatic transcription and recording of the conversation . The message recipients get speech-to-text message readouts via the Alexa app for iOS and Android devices.

Pre-requisites

Here are a few prerequisites for Amazon Calling & Messaging:

- First, you will need an Amazon Echo Plus speaker — the original Echo or the Dot — along with an iOS device (running version 9.0 or higher) or an Android device (running Android 5.0 or higher).
- You will also need a valid phone number.

Setup

- Download the Alexa app for iOS or Android
- Open the Alexa app, and tap the speech bubble icon at the bottom of the screen.
- Here, you'll see a welcome screen. Tap the *Get Started* button.
- Select your name from the list on the following screen. Then, hit the *Continue* button.
- You will be asked to grant Alexa permission to access your phone's contacts. Tap Allow to continue.
- The Alexa app will prompt you to verify your phone number. Enter it, and then wait for the verification code. Paste the code in the corresponding text field and hit the *Continue* button.

Send Voice Message from the Alexa App

- Open the Alexa app, and tap the speech bubble at the bottom of the screen. This will bring up the Conversations screen.
- Tap the person-shaped outline in the upper-right corner of the screen, and choose a person from the resulting list of contacts.

- Tap the message bubble, which will bring up a conversation page with that contact. Then, hit the blue microphone icon to record a voice message. You can also tap the keyboard button to type out a memo.

Start a call from Alexa App

- Open the Alexa app and tap the speech bubble at the bottom of the screen. This brings up the Conversations screen.
- Tap the person-shaped outline in the upper-right corner of the screen, and choose a person from the resulting list of contacts.
- Tap the phone icon, which will initiate the call. It's a little like Skype — the Alexa app uses your phone's microphone and speakers to route voice data over a Wi-Fi or cellular connection, and your voice comes through via the recipient's Echo.

Send a Voice Message from an Echo Plus

- First, make sure the message's intended recipient has enabled Alexa Calling & Messaging by opening the Alexa app, heading to the *Conversations* screen, and tapping the person-shaped outline in the upper-right corner of the screen. If the person has enabled calls and messages, you'll see their name on the resulting list.
- Now say, "Alexa, send a message to [your contact's name here]."

How to Start a call from an Echo Plus

- First, make sure the message's intended recipient has enabled Alexa Calling & Messaging by opening the Alexa app, heading to the Conversations screen, and tapping the person-shaped outline in the upper-right corner of the screen. If the person has enabled calls and messages, you'll see their name on the resulting list.

- Now say, "Alexa, call [your contact's name here]." You'll be connected as soon as your partner answers.

How to Block Calls and Messages

- All you have to do is tap the new "block contact" button near their name, and you won't receive their calls or messages anymore. This update is only available for the iOS version of the Alexa app.

How to Disable Calling and Messaging

- To disable the feature once you've enabled, it, you will have to call the helpline at 1-877-375-9365 or on the Contact Us page, choose Amazon Devices > your Echo name > Echo Devices. Under "Select issue details," choose Something Else, then under "How Would You Like To Contact Us," select Phone. An Amazon employee will call you.

Shopping On Amazon Echo Plus

It is not just about making shopping lists; Echo Plus can also be made use of for placing orders. Not just place orders, it can also help you in looking for alternatives. It can also remember your shopping lists; this feature comes in really handy if you want to reorder something.

If you want to order any supplies for office, you will need to make a list of all the things that you will need to get done. However, with the help of the Echo Plus, you can get it to place the order for the supplies that you require from the Amazon website or app. Then you will need to simply wait for your order to get delivered. You can make changes to or edit an existing order as well. If there are any common orders, then you can get Echo to repeat the same order.

Setup Voice Purchasing

You can buy digital and physical products from Amazon with your Alexa device using the 1-click payment method. You need a US/UK billing address and a payment method and Prime Membership (only for Physical Products) to enable voice transactions. Physical products order is also eligible for free returns.

When you register your Alexa device, Voice Purchasing is on by default.

You can use voice commands to carry out the following activities with your Echo Plus

- **Purchase** a Prime-eligible Item
- **Reorder** an Item
- **Add** an Item to your Amazon cart
- **Track** the Status of a Recently Shipped Item
- **Cancel** an order immediately after ordering it.

To Enable/Disable Voice Purchasing, activate an optional 4-digit confirmation code and check your payment method and billing address

- Open the Alexa App
- Tap Settings
- Voice Purchasing

Now you can access all the purchase settings, to make any required changes.

A few Categories in the physical products are **NOT ELIGIBLE** for voice purchasing.

- Apparel
- Prime Pantry
- Shoes
- Watches
- Prime Now
- Jewellery

- Amazon Fresh
- Add-On items

Now that you are all set for Voice Purchasing!

These are few commands you can use to make your first purchase on Echo Plus.

Alexa Shopping Commands

- *"Alexa, order (item name)"*
- *"Alexa, reorder (item name)"*
- *"Alexa, add (item name) to my cart"*
- *"Alexa, track my order "*
- *"Alexa, where is my stuff?"*
- *"Alexa, cancel my order"*

Buy Music using Echo

To shop for a song or an album use the following commands

- *"Alexa, Shop for the song [song name]"*
- *"Alexa, Shop for the album [album name]"*
- *"Alexa, Shop for the album [artist name]"*

Purchases are stored for free in your music library; they don't count against the storage limits, and are available for playback/download on any device that supports Amazon Music.

Buy Physical Products using Echo Plus

When you make a voice purchase request, Alexa searches through several purchase options

- **Your order history** - (only Prime-eligible items)
- **Amazon's Choice** - (Amazon's Choice items are highly rated, well-priced products with Prime shipping)
- **Prime-eligible items** - (including delivery by Prime Now for eligible items)

If an item is available, Alexa tells you the item name and price. Alexa also tells you the estimated delivery information if it will not be standard Prime 2-day shipping. Additional details about that item are available in the Alexa app. Then, Alexa asks you to confirm or cancel the order.

If Alexa can't find the requested item or can't complete the purchase, Alexa may offer one of these options:

- Add item to cart on Amazon
- Add item to your Alexa Shopping list
- See the Alexa app for more options

You can also ask Alexa to cancel your order immediately after you place it or track your shipped order.

Manage your Shopping/To Do List

You can view up to 100 items on each list. Each list item can be up to 256 characters long. You can also print lists when you view them in a web browser on your computer.

- Tap the main menu on your Alexa App
- Select Shopping & To-do Lists

You can add, remove or edit items on the list in the App itself or by using the voice commands. You can export these lists to Evernote, Gmail, Todoist or iOS Reminders by using IFTTT recipes.

Alexa with Prime Now

Alexa now lets users order anything from its Prime Now retail catalogue, which includes tens of thousands of products including alcohol(in a few cities), as long as you are an Amazon Prime member and live in a Prime Now area. It lets you order multiple items at once, make recommendations and automatically give you the next available two-hour delivery window. Prime Now is currently live in 30 cities, while alcohol delivery is live in just three: Seattle, Washington and Columbus and Cincinnati, Ohio (beer and wine only for the latter two).

You can simply say, "Alexa, please order Doritos from Prime Now," and then Alexa will return results from your history or the best result from a search of the Prime Now catalogue. Once you confirm the item, Alexa will ask if you want to buy more items. In order to meet the minimum order value ($25), Alexa will also provide recommendations for products to buy.

It is worth noting that since Alexa already allowed users to order from Amazon, you need to specify "from Prime Now" when talking to Alexa if you want your order to be delivered in a two-hour window. She will select the next available delivery window for you and place the order. You can choose to add a tip for your courier in the Prime Now app or on the website.

Cancel Order

Simply say "Alexa, cancel my order" within eight seconds of placing the order and your order will be cancelled. You will need to use the Prime Now app to cancel an order after eight seconds. (Go to Your Account, then select Your Orders, and select the order you wish to cancel.) If it can be canceled, you'll see a Cancel Delivery button. You need to contact Customer Service in case you are unable to cancel your order using the app.

Tracking

You need to visit the Prime Now app or website to track your order as Alexa cannot track your Amazon Prime orders.

Where is Prime Now available?

You can only order from Prime Now in the following US cities:

- Atlanta
- Austin
- Baltimore
- Boston
- Charlotte
- Chicago

- Cincinnati
- Columbus
- Dallas and Fort Worth
- Denver
- Houston
- Indianapolis
- Las Vegas
- Los Angeles and Orange County
- Manhattan and Brooklyn
- Miami
- Milwaukee
- Minneapolis and St. Paul
- Nashville
- Orlando
- Phoenix
- Portland
- Raleigh
- Richmond
- Sacramento
- San Antonio
- San Diego
- San Francisco Bay Area
- Seattle and Eastside
- Tampa
- Virginia Beach
- Washington, DC Metro

Please visit the prime now website for an updated list of cities now eligible for Prime Now.

How to Use Alexa with Amazon Wand

How often do you say to yourself, "Oh, I need to get toilet rolls" or "I gotta remember to buy a new light bulbs for the bedroom" and so on? With the Dash Wand, you can simply scan a barcode or press a button to ask Alexa to add that item to your cart.

The Dash Wand is a battery-powered, voice-enabled grocery scanner. Just point it at a barcode and press the button to add that item to your Amazon shopping cart when you're running low on supply, or press and hold to ask Alexa to add it. She'll also talk back to you through the scanner's tiny speaker.

To activate the device, just insert the two included AAA batteries and hold the button down until it enters pairing mode. From there, you'll go to a link on your mobile device that'll sync the Dash Wand up with your Amazon account and your home's Wi-Fi network. You can just stick it to the fridge or hang the Dash Wand from an included stick-up hook.

The Dash Wand can't do everything but it still packs an awful lot of Alexa convenience into a device that practically costs nothing. Prime members who spend purchase the $20 Dash Wand get a $20 Amazon gift card and 90 days of free Amazon Fresh grocery delivery, which normally costs $15 per month.

It can do a few Alexa things, like tell you weather forecasts and silly jokes, it can also do basic math and unit conversions and you can ask how many teaspoons are in a tablespoon etc. She can control your smart home devices or try out third-party Alexa skills. However it has no music, reminders or even kitchen timers, which is disappointing.

Echo Plus in the Kitchen

Alexa is good with controlling smart devices but she is also extremely useful when it comes to helping out in the kitchen by taking hands free commands. She can

- Help create and maintain grocery list
- Convert popular units used in the kitchen
- Step by step walk-through of a recipe
- Timer for food and preparation time
- Make your morning coffee
- Manage larger appliances in the kitchen

Create and Maintain grocery list

Now creating to do and shopping list will be a breeze with simply telling Alexa what you want to add and mention which list it needs to be added to.

For example, if you tell her "Alexa, add milk." As milk is a noun, she will understand that this is an item you want added to your shopping list. You can also tell her "Alexa, please add eggs to my shopping list," or, even use a general command like "Alexa, can you please add an item to my grocery list." For the latter question, Alexa will ask what you want to add and your reply will then be added to your shopping list.

- Alexa, add cheese to my Grocery List.
- Alexa, add eggs to my shopping list.
- Alexa, can you please add an item to my grocery list.
- Alexa, add 'go to the grocery store' to my to-do list.

Convert Units

Imagine you are making preparations for a dinner for 6 and you just found a recipe that serves 4, Alexa can help you convert the recipe for 6 easily. Alexa also can convert units, which is a handy function when you are busy cooking and your hands are covered in four or meat. Alexa can answer basic conversion questions without any skill enhancement.

- Alexa, convert 2 cups to milliliters.
- Alexa, convert this recipe for 4 people.
- Alexa, how many teaspoons are in 3 tablespoons?

Start a timer/ alarm

Just say Alexa please start a timer for 15 minutes. After 15 minutes, she will chime until you ask her to stop. Set multiple timers and she can manage them at ease. Also check with her how much time is left asking or cancel a timer that is no longer needed.

You can also start an alarm for either a specific time or one that is relative. For example you can say "Alexa, Please set an alarm for 5 a.m." or you can tell her "Alexa, Please set an alarm clock for 30 minutes from now "

- Alexa, how much time is left on the pizza timer?
- Alexa, remind me to check the oven in 5 minutes.

- Alexa, set a pizza timer for 20 minutes.
- Alexa, cancel the pizza timer.

Pair wine with food

With Alexa's help you can not only cook the food but also find a good wine to go with it. Wine Buddy is a wine and food pairing skill that gives you pairing options based on what you ask.

- Alexa, ask Wine Buddy what I should pair with salmon.
- Alexa, what can I serve with steak?

Calorie count

Besides using Alexa for recipes you can also use it to track calories. Although it does not know all of the complex and unique foods that exist, it does know the basics. Alexa can provide all the available nutritional information it has.

- Alexa, ask calorie counter to log food apple.
- Alexa, ask calorie counter how many calories I've had today.
- Alexa, ask calorie counter to delete my last food.
- Alexa, Ask food tracker how many calories are in 2 eggs and 3 slices of bacon?
- Alexa, Ask food tracker how many carbs are in 3 ounces of pasta?
- Alexa, ask food tracker for my calorie report.

Cocktail recipe ideas

If you're not into wine, there are a number of skills that will provide cocktail recipes. Have guests over and you are clueless as to where you should begin. Just ask Alexa to open up Easy Cocktail. Ask her for a specific cocktail and she will list down the ingredients and the step-by-step instructions.

Have a specific liquor at home that you want use, just ask Alexa to open the Bartender and ask for recommendations.

- Alexa, open Easy Cocktail.

- Alexa, ask Easy Cocktail how I can make an Old Fashioned.
- Alexa, ask Easy cocktail how to make a sex on the beach.

Allrecipes

Get access to 60,000 Plus of America's most loved recipes from Allrecipes.com. No need anymore to type, tap, swipe or squint to get the best recipes your family would enjoy. Just as Alexa and get the dinner ready in a breeze.

The Allrecipes Skill gives you the convenience of hands-free access to recipes be it for everyday dinners or dinner for family and friends. Alexa can help you quickly find recipes that meet your requirements - be it preferred cooking method, available cooking time, type of dish you would like to make or ingredients you have on hand. Alexa can help save recipes to Allrecipes Favorites and retrieve recipes later as needed. Ask Alexa to send the recipe to your phone, so you can quickly make a trip to the store for the ingredients. Want to give the recipe a new twist, Alexa can share what variations other cooks have made by sharing reviews with you.

You will need to provide her with your phone number (if you want recipes sent to your phone) and Allrecipes login information (if you want to retrieve or add recipes to favorites.

- Alexa, Open Allrecipes. (Opens the Allrecipes Skill)
- Alexa, ask Allrecipes what can I make with bacon, chicken and cheddar cheese?
- Alexa, Ask Allrecipes to find me the recipe for World's Best Pizza.
- Alexa, ask Allrecipes for a slow cooker recipe for pulled pork.
- Alexa, Ask Allrecipes to find me a chocolate chip cookie recipe from my Favorites.
- Alexa, ask Allrecipes for the recipe of the day?"
- Alexa, add this recipe to my Favorites.
- Alexa, tell me the reviews for this recipe.
- Alexa, send the recipe to my phone.
- Alexa, what ingredients are needed for this recipe?
- Alexa, open All Recipes and find me a chicken recipe that takes less than 45 minutes.
- Alexa, Ask All Recipes the next step.
- Alexa, send the recipe to my phone.

Control large appliances

Wouldn't it be nice if you could get out of bed and simply tell Alexa to make your coffee? You can! Simply utilize a smart switch and IFTTT programming. Simply remember your trigger phrase in the morning and you are good to go.

You can also control things like your dishwasher, oven or even your slow cooker with your Alexa enabled device.

Generate recipe ideas

Aside from the All Recipes skill, there are a number of skills that allow for the finding of recipes using your Amazon Echo or Amazon Echo These skills include:

Recipe Finder by Ingredient

- Alexa, ask Recipe Finder by Ingredient what I can make with chicken and corn
- Alexa, ask Recipe Finder by Ingredient what kind of sandwich can I make with cheddar cheese
- Alexa, ask Recipe Finder by Ingredient to find me a recipe with eggs, condensed milk, and pumpkin.
- Alexa, ask Recipe Finder by Ingredient what can I make with chicken with mushrooms?

Trending Recipes & Food

- Alexa, can you get the latest recipe from Trending Recipes?
- Alexa, can I have the fifth recipe from Trending Recipes?
- Alexa, can you give me the most recent recipe in Trending Recipes?

Best Recipes

- Alexa, ask best recipes what's for dinner
- Alexa, open Best Recipes

Step by Step walk through for recipes

- Alexa, show me a slow cooker recipe from Allrecipes.
- Alexa, find me a pie recipe.
- Alexa, search for Chef John's Pumpkin Pie.
- Alexa, reviews.
- Alexa, how much time does the recipe take?
- Alexa, what is the recipe of the day?
- Alexa, recipe details.
- Alexa, find me a pumpkin pie recipe.
- Alexa, find me the Perfect Pumpkin Pie recipe

Make Alexa Your Smart Home Hub

Wouldn't it be awfully convenient if you could have voice control over the lights, locks, and temperature in the house? Perhaps even things like the oven temperature and the cooking time? Echo Plus can handle smart lights, locks, can open and close garage doors, and control the temperature in the house as well.

Connect Smart Devices at HOME

To build your Smart Home, you no longer need a 3rd party smart home hub. Echo Plus can control all the ZigBee smart devices directly through the built-in ZigBee Smart Home Hub. Moreover Echo Plus can also connect with hundreds of WiFi and Bluetooth enabled smart devices just like the other Echo family devices. ZigBee is an open source protocol that is used by hundreds of Smart Home devices eg. Phlips Hue Light and Smart Locks.

However please remember that not all smart devices are ZigBee powered. If you already have a Smart Home, please check out the compatibility of all your smart devices with Echo Plus. Because to control certain devices you may still need a 3rdparty Smart Home Hub.

To setup a new Smart Home Device just say-

"Alexa, discover my devices"

Echo Plus will discover all the compatible devices and set them up automatically. For a list of Echo Plus compatible ZigBee Smart Devices please checkout Simple Setup devices Compatible with Echo Plus at Amazon.com.

This feature would alone save you plenty of time and effort going back and forth and downloading a new app for each smart device family and integrating that with your Alexa app.

Devices Directly Controlled by Alexa

Following are few of the Smart Devices that can be directly controlled by Alexa via Wifi. (For a comprehensive list please refer to Appendix A1)

Lighting and Fans

- LIFX Wifi Smart LED Light Bulbs
- Haiku Wifi Ceiling Fans

Switches and Outlets

- Belkin WeMo: Light Switch, Switch (Smart Plug) and Insight Switch
- TP-Link: Smart Plug and Smart Plug with Energy Monitoring
- D-Link Wifi Smart Plugs

Thermostats

- Nest Learning Thermostat
- Ecobee3 Smarter Wifi Thermostat
- Sensi Wifi Programmable Thermostat

Locks

- Garageio
- Danalock

Car Control

- Automatic

Control Your Smart Devices using Amazon Echo Plus

Basic Voice Commands

The following list of commands works really well with Alexa and have been tested.

ON Commands

- "Alexa, turn on <Device Name>"
- "Alexa, start <Device Name>"
- "Alexa, unlock <Device Name>"
- "Alexa, open <Device Name>"
- "Alexa, boot up <Device Name>"
- "Alexa, run <Device Name>"
- "Alexa, arm <Device Name>"

OFF Commands

- "Alexa, turn off <Device Name>"
- "Alexa, stop <Device Name> (this one is tricky to get right)"
- "Alexa, stop running <Device Name> (also very tricky)"
- "Alexa, lock <Device Name>"
- "Alexa, close <Device Name>"
- "Alexa, shutdown <Device Name>"
- "Alexa, shut <Device Name>"
- "Alexa, disarm <Device Name>"

DIM Commands

- "Alexa, brighten <Device Name> to <Position>"
- "Alexa, dim <Device Name> to <Position>"
- "Alexa, raise <Device Name> to <Position>"
- "Alexa, lower <Device Name> to <Position>"

- "Alexa, set <Device Name> to <Position>"
- "Alexa, turn up <Device Name> to <Position>"
- "Alexa, turn down <Device Name> to <Position>"

Advanced Voice Commands to Control your Smart Devices

- "Alexa, turn off/on the bedroom light"
- "Alexa, brighten/dim the kitchen light"
- "Alexa set the bedroom light to 12 (Brightness scale of 0 - 100.)"
- "Alexa, lower/raise kitchen thermostat by 15 degrees"
- "Alexa, set kitchen thermostat to 74 degrees"

Alexa Routines

Routines is a feature recently launched by Amazon. It is pre-programing a list of actions that will be performed by Alexa at specific times or on specific commands. So instead of giving multiple commands for each small task you need to say a trigger phase and all the commands will be performed in a sequence.

To Setup a Routine follow these instuctions:

- Go To the Alexa app
- Tap the Menu button on the Top Left.
- Select the Settings.
- Scroll down and tap Accounts.
- Inside Accounts Tap Routines.
- Tap on the plus (+) in the top-right hand corner.
- Tap When this happens.
- Select When you say something or select At a scheduled time.
- If you selected When you say something, type in a phrase, such as "Good morning" or "Movie time."
- If you selected At a scheduled time, set a time and choose which days it should repeat.
- Click Done.

- Now, tap Add action.
- Click Add to add an action and repeat the same process until all the desired actions are added.
- Now, choose which speaker the routine will play audio from. If you use a scheduled routine, you will have to select a speaker, but if you create a routine based on a phrase, you can specify that you want it to play audio from whichever speaker you speak to.
- To finish setting up a routine, click Create.

Please note that for actions, you can only choose Smart Home actions, News, Traffic and Weather. This is a new feature and once rolled out, more actions will be a part of the routines.

Grouping Smart Devices Together

Suppose after working in the attic you are tired and getting ready for bed, you want to switch off the lights. Not only those on the top floor, but also those in the porch and the hallway. One easy hack is to Group the desired Smart Home Devices together and then you can control them with a simple command like "Alexa, turn on (group name)"

Please note that your Echo Plus can be a part of one smart home group at a time.

To create a smart home group, follow these steps:

- Open Alexa App
- Go to the **Menu**
- Select **Smart Home**
- Select **Groups**
- Select **Add Group**
- Select the group type:
  - **Smart Home Group**: Turn devices on/off, lock, and more.
  - **Multi-Room Music Group**: Stream the same music station, song, or playlist to compatible devices.

- Enter a **name** for the group you created.
- Select the smart devices you want to add to the group
- Select **Save**

Once you do this, just command Alexa.

- "Alexa, turn on (group name)"

In this way, you can schedule a program to turn off the lights or use a single voice command such as, "Alexa, turn off all the lights" just before you go to bed.

Alexa Scenes

Building a Smart Home is all about automating your errands at home. Image the color temperature in your living room changing as soon as you switch on your TV. Certain smart devices have pre-scripted behavior and trigger actions that happen as soon as certain conditions are met. But the challenge is that these scripts are not a part of the Alexa universe.

Alexa Scenes is a way to integrate these smart actions within the Alexa eco-system. So instead of going to each individual device app and activating these scripts, Alexa collects these scripts and lets you use voice command to activate them.

Setup Scenes:

- Open Alexa App
- Tap on **Menu**
- Tap **Smart Home**
- Tap **Scenes**.
- Tap **Discover**
- Wait for Alexa to scan for devices with Scenes
- Once a discovery is made, Go To the device app and Tap **Sync** the give Alexa access to those scenes.

How to Use Yonomi with Alexa

Alexa seems somewhat reluctant clubbing the Switch ON and Switch OFF routines. You must write the programs separate and hope that they work. But, by combining Yonomi with Alexa you get a lot more things done.

The way to do this is to create the routines first in Yonomi. Name this with the room name say, Hall. In this, you turn on the Sonos, the light bulbs, and the fan. After you have done this, you do the turn off routine where you stop Sonos and turn off the light bulb and fan. Name this as Hall Off. When you turn on Amazon Echo Plus discovery, it will map both these events to one device. Now, you can use Echo Plus to turn on the hall lights with "Alexa, turn ON Hall" and then turn them off with "Alexa, turn OFF Hall." Simple!

Setting up Alexa through Yonomi

- Open the Yonomi app
- Tap on the icon present at the top left corner
- You must now select the Accounts and Hubs Tab.
- Tap at the bottom right-hand corner (upper right-hand corner if you use iOS).
- Now choose Amazon Echo Plus Account.
- Give your password and access your account.
- Now click on Connect.

Now use Echo to tell "Alexa, discover my devices." There you are, all done.

Alexa as Your child's Bedtime Assistant

Room filling sound with crisp vocals
and dynamic bass response

Bedtime timer

To help children adjust to a good bedtime routine it is important for them to understand and accept the fact that bedtime is approaching. Instead of you holding the timer and playing the bad mama or bad dad, you can ask Alexa to set a timer for you. Your children can even ask Alexa how many more minutes they have until bedtime.

Read your little one a bedtime story

Try getting Alexa to help in the bedtime routine while you are busy brushing your teeth or getting ready for bed yourself.

- She can connect to your Audible.com account and will read them stories available in your account.
- Alexa can use the skill - "Short Bedtime Story" to tell a personalized story to your children. She can tell a story to them personalized for them, with their name mentioned at various points. You can also customize and disable stories you do not want your children to hear and create new ones tailored to your family.

For example - When you say "Alexa, please tell Bedtime Story to Henry"

She will start narrating a story like..."Once upon a time there was a magical wizard named Henry who came upon a little frog with blond hair. Henry asked the frog..."

- Alexa, tell Bedtime Story to Allie
- Alexa, launch Bedtime Story
- Alexa, ask Bedtime Story to Configure

Play a few lullabies

Create a bedtime Lullaby playlist online so that Alexa can play it whenever you ask her to. What a great way to end a bedtime routine with a song each night!

Dim the lights

If you have the right light bulbs and dimmer switches in your child's room / nursery, you can just Ask Alexa to dim the lights once the bedtime routine nears an end.

White noise machine

Alexa can play your child white noise, although this does mean you will need to leave the device in the child's room / nursery and that may not be practical for your family.

Integrating Alexa with IFTTT

IFTTT interface provides the easiest way to link various apps and functions with Alexa.

There are plenty of IFTTT recipes that you can use with Echo Plus to automate your life and carry out repeatable tasks to save time and effort. But first you need to connect your Amazon account with IFTTT.

- Go to IFTTT and setup an account if you don't have one
- Go to channels home page and select Amazon Alexa channel
- This will prompt you to enter your Amazon account info to sign in
- Once your sign in you can access all the existing recipes for Alexa

- Choose from among 800+ recipes and add them to your account

Smart Home Recipes in IFTTT

Temperature Control with Nest Thermometer

You choose a phrase and the temperature you want. Then, you say,

- "Alexa, set [phrase]"

And your room temperature is set according to your wish.

For doing this, first, go to the IFTTT and connect to the respective Nest channel.

- Open the Amazon Alexa Channel with your smartphone or computer.
- To do this, click on the three horizontal lines on the top left corner.
- Scroll down and choose Smart Home option.
- You come to the Device Links tab.
- Under this select Nest and click Continue.
- Log in with the Nest id and password.
- Now, you see Discover Devices.
- If Nest is on the local Wi-Fi network, Alexa will discover it.

You set the phrase to change the temperature

- "Alexa, set room temperature to 74 degrees now"

Automate your Life with SIGNUL Beacon channel

It is an amazingly unique way of creating a bridge between your physical and digital world just by detecting the presence or absence of your smartphone.

Define your zone entry and exit events to Signul Beacon to help automate mundane tasks. The Channel will use your physical context to streamline your digital world.

Here are things you can do once this you fix up this channel.

- Upon reaching your desk, you are logged into a spread sheet
- Slack is informed when you arrived for work
- When you arrive home, turn on the lights
- At bedtime, mute phone
- When you leave work, turn on Nest thermostat

To execute these hacks, connect to Signul Beacon Channel on your IFTTT account and start using it.

House lights go on at sunset

Set your lights to go off at sunrise and on at sunset by the use of WeMo switches. You can control one or a group of lights and since they do not require batteries as they are Wifi controlled, they can operate forever. You can use any brand of light, fluorescent, halogen, LED, incandescent, and fans with the WeMo switch. The program works well even if you experience a power outage. However, you cannot replace three-way switches.

Download the WeMo app from Google Play or iOS for your Smart phone. You can turn on WeMo or turn it off. But first, you have to connect the Wink Relay Channel and the WeMo Switch Channel on IFTTT. While we are here, you should know that Wink Relay channel fits well with WeMo switches, Android SMS, Tesco, Sensibo, Yo and EVE for Tesla.

Turn Hue Lamps Red or Green

Magic begins when you change the ambiance with just a single command. Alexa will turn your Philips Hue Lamp Green, Red or turn them off when you want. But, connect the Philips Hue Channel and your IFTTT Workflow Channel first.

Adding Devices

If you haven't done so already, here are devices you can add to your smart home. You will find all these under WeMo and devices in IFTTT

WeMo Devices

- Crockpot: You can add two different commands: one to cook slow and the other to turn it off. This helps you control your crockpot.
- Maker: With this you can turn on, turn off and let the appliance run for a while. You must set the appropriate command as "Alexa, turn on (off) the sprinklers" or "Alexa, set pool pump for 20."
- Coffeemaker: This helps you brew coffee.
- Switch: Plug any device you wish to control into the WeMo Switch such as turn on a lamp in the morning at 7 AM or turn on lights when I arrive home.

Sonos

- "Alexa, play the front room Sonos"
- "Alexa, set my living room Sonos to 40"

Quirky Aros

- "Alexa, turn on Aros"
- "Alexa, turn off Aros"
- "Alexa, set Aros to 80"

Music Recipes in IFTTT

IFTTT Integration for Music

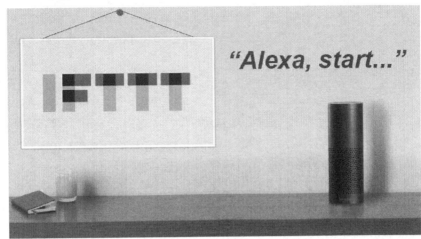

Gone are the touch and gestures to control your smartphone, your room air-conditioner, and those lights. Say it and Echo Plus will do it. Gone too are the days when all you could do is wish that the boring music would stop. Now you can and switch to a channel that has your kind of music playing.

Music is only as good as its clarity. Listen to a bunch of vague sounds without a beat or harmony and you will get a headache. This is why music lovers attempt to ensure their selection has the right sound and the right mood.

Set up the smart Hi-Fi system in every room. Connect to Musaic to improve the sound quality of your music. If you connect the lights to Music, you will get party lights when the music begins. Also, you can wake up with music streaming and night-lights fade.

And don't miss out on the Deezer channel. With Deezer, you can take your music with you to every place you go. Use Add new tracks to make a fast addition of the tracks you want to Deezer.

- Sync your favorite songs to SoundCloud
- Add artist
- List favorite songs on Evernote

- Listen to favorites from SoundCloud on Deezer
- Add favorite to Google spread sheet

Connect to music with Musixmatch

Connect your favorite songs to Musixmatch.

Spotify Playlist

For those who have an Apple account, you can create a Spotify playlist from your Apple Music Playlist. Connect to Spotify Channel and Workflow Channel to execute this.

SoundCloud

This app SoundCloud has many recipes that give music a new meaning. Share your SoundCloud tracks to Facebook; sync them to your Spotify collection; Use Genius to follow the songs you like on SoundCloud or share new songs to Tumblr.

Work recipes in IFTTT

How to Note events with precise time and people on your calendar

First, go with your mobile or computer browser and connect the Google channel. To improve on this functionality, use the Slack channel to connect this note with every member of your team or family. An alternate way to do this is to go to Amazon Alexa settings. Click on Calendar and pen in a new event.

How to Schedule for Repeated Tasks

Improve your schedule with the Google Calendar and your regular schedule. Do this daily or once every week to create more thinking space and organize your work schedule. For this, the Trello channel will not only serve as a reminder for these repeating tasks but also help you make plans.

How To Share your workflow with the iOS phone

Create a workflow and connect the Workflow Channel and Google Drive Channel. This now enables you to share a web page or text with Google Doc. If you use Slack, then you may send your message or web page. The two channels to connect are Slack Channel and Workflow Channel.

How To Set up DocSend Channel

Use this channel to keep track of the documents you send. Connect to various recipes and get informed when any person reads 100% of your document, post message to Slack channel whenever you have a new visit to a document, get an email of all the 100% document reads, remind me to follow up when someone reads 100% of my document (this could be your family member reading a family update) and much more. You can add this channel to these given here.

- **If Channel**: You can use the Get Notifications from the If Channel if someone visits and reads 100% of your document.
- **FollowUp.cc**: This helps our intrepid blogger or businessperson to keep 'with it'. You follow-up and see the reads. Connect first to start at this site.
- **Slack**: Post to the Slack Channel if you get a new visitor and if anyone reads 100% of your document.
- **ORBneXt**: In this, your Orb will flash when you have a visitor or anyone reads through the entire document.
- **Gmail**: This is the most popular internet device and you can connect DocSend channel to improve communications. You will get an email when you have a visitor.

How To Setup a Square Channel

Square gives you the best way to allow payments by credit cards on your site. To activate this, you need to create a Square account. You can use the connected services related to sales and payment.

- **Refunds**: When someone uses Square to make a new refund this adds a new line to your spreadsheet. Or better, you can receive an email to any account when you receive a refund over a specified amount.
- **Payments**: You get an email when money is credited to your Square account.
- **Funds heading into account**: Likewise, you can get a notification when funds are heading towards your account.

Square channel fits well with all the channels mentioned for the DocSend Channel such as ORBneXt and Gmail.

How to Integrate Blogging networks

Use one or many of the blog channels such as Blogger, WordPress, or Tumblr. You can add your business network when you use LinkedIn, Square, Slack, Quip or Salesforce.

- Tumblr: With Tumblr, you can post your Instagram photos to your Tumblr blog. Further, you can publish selected Flickr images as Tumblr posts.
- Blogger: Here you can use many recipes to add content to your Blogger. For instance, Blog my Dropbox images and Share my new posts to Facebook provide an easy means to achieve your aim. Other people Push sweet Vimeo videos to my Blogger.
- WordPress: WordPress is the favorite for many bloggers since it is stable and easy to use. Here with Echo, things have turned easier. The various recipes such as WP to Tumblr, Upload YouTube videos to WP blog, and Instagram to Blog help you publish your articles on the Internet with ease.

How to Speed up Complex Actions using Launch Center

Through this channel, you can add speed to your tasks. Launch Center Pro saves time by doing complex actions with a single command. You can use it to launch the Waze app when you leave home

- First get the Waze app.
- Set Launch Center Pro to get notifications.
- Now, you are ready to connect to the Launch Center Channel.

How To Connect Fitbit through IFTTT

Go to this website and connect the two channels given there, the Fitbit channel and Google Calendar channel. Now, Alexa will remind you to go to sleep on time and adjust your sleep schedule according to the quality of sleep recorded the previous night. And you have your activity on a Google Spreadsheet.

Using Alexa Skills on Echo Plus

Alexa SKILL Commands

Your Amazon Echo comes with a set of built in abilities. To enhance these abilities or to add new abilities to your Echo Plus add new Alexa Skills that are developed by Amazon or third party Skills developers. You can find these Skills on your Alexa App.

These skills are the Alexa equivalent of iOS/Android Apps for your Smart Phone. Alexa Skills development is still in its infancy but this platform is developing fast. As more and more people buy Echo Plus and Amazon launches it in multiple countries, you will see a sudden surge in the number of skills for Alexa.

All skills support Launch command and Stop command and majority support the Help command.

Launch

Just say....

- "Alexa, launch [skill name]"

The skill will be launched and you will come to know that hearing the welcome message for the particular skill. Some information about the skill and applicable sample commands will be included in the message.

Stop

This one is straightforward. One quick hack: you can actually say *"Alexa, Stop"* even when Echo is speaking. Just be loud enough so that Alexa is able to hear you out over her voice.

Help

Most of the Alexa Skills have a help function except some Skills, which are pretty straightforward. To access this help, just say, "Help," and Alexa will read out the particular Skill's Help file to you.

Alexa Skills for Smart Home Control

Alexa Skills are like Apps for your Echo Plus that you can use to carry out advanced controls from your Echo Plus.

Grouping your devices

If you have a SmartHome, *Group* the devices first. Through the *Group* Alexa will control operations of your SmartHome. Connect the apps you already have. Each of these apps will have a set of commands. For instance, Alexa controls LIFX lights with commands such as, *"Alexa turn the lights on," "Alexa, dim bedroom lights by 25%,"* or *"Alexa, Turn Kitchen light off."*

Nest

You may find that Alexa does not discover your Nest apps unless you name them right when you start. Use the term 'set' and then 'thermostat' (rename your thermostat to 'thermostat' if you have another name for it) and then call out the command. *'Alexa, set the thermostat to 80 degrees,'* or *'Alexa, cool down the master bedroom'* and so on.

Harmony

This app lets you group and name activities in your home. You can combine thermostats, lights, television, movies, blinds, or music. After grouping activities you can use a variety of commands such as *"Alexa, Start Harmony Activity"*, *"Alexa, End Harmony Activity"*, and *"Alexa, Use location to start Harmony Activity"*.

Smart Things

Much similar to Harmony, the SmartThings app lets you control electronics, lights, and everyday events with your smartphone. You can unlock the door with #hashtag, turn on a light when WeMo detects motion, get a phone call when SmartThings detect moisture.

Integrate with Home Control Assistant

The Home Control Assistant (HCA) links well with Alexa. At present, it has many features that work without Alexa but it helps improve your SmartHome. These are features apart from voice control for Alexa such as control for iPad, Windows, Android and iPhone. HCA helps you run several instances that involve the state of your house, location, time and event into one program. To do this, go to alexa.amazon.com and click on **Enable Skill**.

EventSeeker

For people who like action, EventSeeker helps them narrow things down with the help of Alexa. Alexa will read out the events in the category of your choice and you can find out what is happening in your locality and when it occurs. You do not have to sweat to find out the events you would like to attend. It's as simple as eating pie.

Track your things

Use a mix of *TrackR Bravo Tags* and *TrackR Atlas Plugs* to find things like your purse, keychain, car keys or your pet cat. *TrackR Atlas Plugs* map the house. You place *TrackR Bravo Tags* on selected items. Once you do this, you can find these items by asking Alexa, *"Alexa, where are my car keys?"* and you get, *"Your car keys are on the living room sofa."* While the *Atlas Plugs* cost $39 per piece the *Tags* cost $29 each.

Alexa Skills for Exercise

For fitness freaks and exercise enthusiasts, there is a host of apps you can access.

Connect with Fitbit

Use Fitbit to update your daily fitness goals. Though not as interactive as you would like it to be, Fit Assist will tell you interesting facts on health and fitness upon request.

Amazon and Alexa do not store the data about your exercises but you use the interactions to update your goals daily. You will find this under skills in the alexa.amazon.com site.

Use the FitnessLogger

This Alexa skill helps you record your fitness schedule you follow. You can compare your workout you did the previous day and save the workout you did today. *"Alexa, ask FitnessLogger for all supported exercises"* will give you a list of workable exercises. Go to your Alexa app, to enable this skill.

7-Minute Workout

This skill helps you lower stress and cut fat. Enable this and use commands such as *"Alexa, start seven-minute workout"* or *"Alexa, start Workout."*

Training Tips

This set of tips helps the newcomers orient themselves to the gym workout. Enable this skill and use a command such as *"Alexa, ask Training Tips for tips today."*

Recon Channel

Recon app is expensive but one of the trending eyewear technology to boost your connectivity. Meant for the Sports and Fitness category, you can get metrics projected to your eyepiece. This way you do not have to break your routine activity but you read the information. In this way, you can get news, calendar notifications, DubNation updates, sports news, and updates from your smartphone too. The unit costs $499 on Amazon. One may extend the capabilities of this app when you connect to third party apps with ANT+. Use the camera to get instant snaps of real events.

ALOP-Pilates-Class-Skill

This skill helps beginners to work out their Pilates exercises. *"Alexa, start Pilates class"* will take you through the exercise schedule. But first, you must enable this skill. Go to ALotOfPilates.com to get more details on the exercises.

Alexa Skills for Music

This section has plenty of apps and one only needs the time to go through it. Here we list some important ones that would be of interest. Add the stations to Echo Plus and you have a good selection of songs to listen to all the time.

Fluffy Radio

A favorite with radio music listeners, Fluffy Radio helps you make requests and stream the songs through TuneIn. *"Alexa, ask Fluffy Radio to request Silent Night."* Or, *"Alexa, open Fluffy Radio."* This is a fun way to listen to songs.

Spotify Premium

You have to sign up and buy one of their music packs. This monthly pack starts at $19 and goes on to $29, $59.99 and $79.99.

Tune your Guitar

This is an amazingly handy Skill. Just follow these steps and your will have a tuned guitar.

- In the Alexa Skills menu, search for Guitar Tuner.
- Use the following command, "Alexa, ask Guitar Tuner to tune my guitar."
- The tuning will start in the following tone sequence: from low E to high E and everything in-between.
- Tune until you have and tuned Guitar.

Play Games with Echo Plus

Alexa is known for its smart-home, news, music and productivity skills but if you thought she was all work and no play then you are, mistaken. She is full of wit and jokes and has a great sense of humor. She is a good games master and capable of playing games and can make your dinner parties a hit. Be it interactive stories or new round of Jeopardy or a round of Bingo, Amazon's voice assistant can keep you entertained for hours. Below are listed some of the best trivia and games skills for Alexa.

The Magic Door

It is an interactive "choose your own adventure" game using Alexa. There are at present nine stories to choose from including saving monkeys on a tropical island, helping the princess find her crown, helping gnome find a key or exploring a witch's spooky mansion. The story unfolds based on the choices you make and Alexa describes the scene as you go along .The game is targeted towards younger ears and as each story is only 5 to 10 minutes long it is very effective if you are trying to get the kids quickly to bed.

To get started, just say, "Alexa, enable The Magic Door".

The Wayne Investigation

The Wayne Investigation is another choose your own adventure game for Alexa .You need to investigate the death of Thomas and Martha Wayne - Bruce Wayne's parents. The choices you make will decide the course of your investigation and affect your ability to solve the mystery. It is a great game for fans of the Dark Knight although it does contains some content that may not be suitable for all ages.

Start the game by saying, "Alexa, open The Wayne Investigation" and follow the prompts.

Earplay

Earplay are thriller stories with an interactive twist where you play the part of a secret agent in a radio drama. As is with other choose your own adventure games the choices you make determines how the story unfolds.

Blackjack

You can now play numerous rounds of Blackjack with Alexa with the skill- Beat The Dealer. You can ask Alexa to read the rules or ask her to give you basic game strategy. You can also ask her to "deal", and then "hit" or "stand" as you choose. She will tell you what the dealer chose and whether it busted or you won the game. The result is recorded whether you won or lost. You can at any time check with Alexa if you won more than you lost. As the games can go on forever remember to say "Alexa, stop" to interrupt and get on with the game.

To enable of a game of blackjack simply say the following commands,

"Alexa, start a game of blackjack" or "Alexa, open The Dealer."

Christmas Kindness

One of the most positive skill alexa has to offer is Christmas Kindness. She will give you a daily suggestion of how you can be kind during the holiday season. Start your day with by simply saying, "Alexa, Open Christmas Kindness" and she will provide you a random idea about how to integrate kindness into your daily life this holiday season.

Alexa Easter Eggs

Though the future is far away, there is no reason for us to not use the future technology today. Alexa may need to cover many more milestones to achieve perfection but the state it made is good enough. After all, one can search and find Easter eggs that the bunny (Alexa) has hidden away.

Fun Phrases to Try Out with Echo Plus

Here is a list of fun phrases you can try out with Echo Plus. This list has been compiled from various sources on the net and is not an exhaustive list as Alexa development team keeps on publishing more phrases regularly.

- What is your favorite color?
- Do you have a boyfriend?
- Where do babies come from?
- Which comes first; chicken or egg?
- Do aliens exist?
- Where do you live?
- Do you want to build a snowman?
- What is love?
- Who won best actor Oscar in 1973?
- May the force be with you!
- Who let the dogs out?
- To be or not to be?
- Who loves ya baby?
- Who is the walrus?
- How tall are you?
- Where are you from?
- Do you want to fight?
- Do you want to play a game?
- I think you are funny?
- Is the cake a lie?
- Random fact
- Roll a dice
- Tell me a joke
- Mac or PC?
- Give me a hug
- Are you lying?
- How many angels can dance?
- I want the truth
- What's in the name?
- Knock knock
- What are you wearing?
- Rock paper scissors
- Party time

- Make me breakfast
- Where are my keys?
- Do you know the way to San Jose?
- Party on, Wayne
- Beam me up
- Make me sandwich
- How much does the earth weigh?
- Tea. Earl Grey. Hot.
- Who is your daddy?
- Is there Santa?
- Best Tablet
- When is the end of the world?
- How many roads must a man walk down?
- Count by Ten
- Can you give me some Money? (Ask twice)
- Do you believe in ghosts?
- Do you believe in god?
- Do you believe in life after love?
- Do you know Siri?
- Do you like green eggs and ham?
- Do you really want to hurt me?
- Fire photon torpedoes
- Good night
- High five!
- How do I get rid of a dead body?
- Do you make bread?
- How many calories are in (name a food)?
- Live long and prosper
- Never gonna give you up
- One fish, two fish
- I'm home
- I've fallen and I can't get up
- I am your father
- I have seen things you people wouldn't believe.
- Tell me a story

- Will you marry me?

Special Animal Sounds

Meantime, you can have loads of fun with special music and soundtracks. Amazon Prime members have access to this while non-members have to pay $0.89 for each track of animal sounds. The tracks themselves are interesting and you should look at the customer reviews of each one before you purchase them. You can get the best ones that way with ease. The collections include bird sounds (favorite with nature lovers and meditation freaks), animal sounds ("Alexa, what did the dog say this morning") and various mixes.

Maker Channel

If you want to get involved in this product, you can do it via the Maker Channel. You may connect your DIY project to this channel to share your experience with others. Go to *huckster.Io* to share your experience with others.

Reset, Change Settings and Troubleshooting

Change the Wake Word

The default wake word is ALEXA.

You can choose from among four of the following wake words.

- Alexa
- Echo
- Amazon
- Computer

To change is wake word on your mobile or computer

- Open Alexa app.
- Go to the control panel.
- On the left, you will see a list.
- Select **Settings** for the Echo device for which you want to change the 'wake word'.
- You will see Wake Word listed for each device.
- Click on this and select the new 'wake word'.
- Now click **Save.**
- This change is possible only on Echo and Echo Plus.

Working with the Remote

Remote does not come in the Echo box but can be purchased separately.

The remote has a microphone, a talk button, and Playback controls. To talk, you press the talk button and talk. The playback button helps you to Play or Pause, Increase or Decrease the Volume, and switch to Next or Previous. The advantage when you use the remote is that you need not 'wake' up Alexa with the 'wake word'. This proves invaluable for those who have more than one Echo units and do not want to disturb the one on the top floor when 'talking' the one in your living room.

Reset to Factory Default

If you are having trouble with your Echo Plus you can restart your device to see if it resolves your problem. To restart your Amazon Echo Plus,

- Unplug the 9W power adapter from the back of the device or from the wall outlet.
- Then, re plug the power adapter.

If this does not solve your problem then you can follow the steps mentioned to reset your Echo Plus.

To **Reset** your Echo Plus:

There's a tiny buttonhole that is present near the bottom of the device, besides the plug. You will need to insert a pin and press this button for resetting the device. The light ring will turn orange and then turn blue. This means that your Echo Plus has been reset. You can turn it off and turn it on again till the light ring on top turns white and cyan.

How to Enforce Updates of Software

Your Echo receives software updates automatically on Wifi

To determine the current software version for your Alexa device in the Alexa app:

- Open the left navigation panel, and then select Settings.
- Select your device, and then scroll down until you see Device software version.

The Alexa software is updated periodically on its own, but

sometimes there can be a delay between the release of new updates and your device receiving them. In such a scenario you can force update by keeping the Echo Plus on MUTE for 30 minutes. When you switch it on again, your Echo Plus would be updated.

Is Alexa Spying On You?

No. Alexa is not spying on you. Alexa only pays attention to you when it hears the designated wake word. Rest of the time, although technically it is on all the time and always on a look out for the wake word from you, it does not record your voice.

But if you are still worried that Alexa will hear and record any private conversations, you can push MUTE button and Echo Plus will not hear or follow anything you say.

How to Ensure Alexa Stops Listening

Press the MUTE button on top of the Echo Plus. The top LED ring will turn red when the mute is ON. You can unmute by pressing the same button again.

There have been zero cases of people using Echo Plus for illegal activities till date. However, to take further precaution and prevent any kind of monkey business from your Echo Plus device ensure that you:

- Do not position the Amazon Echo Plus near any window.

- Do not position the Echo Plus close to any speakerphone or answering machine.
- Mute your Amazon Echo Plus device when away from home.

Amazon's official response to privacy concerns as follows:

"Echo only streams recordings from the user's home when the 'wake word' activates the device, though the device is technically capable of streaming voice recordings at all times, and in fact will always be listening to detect if a user has uttered the word."[1]

However you need to know that Echo Plus uses machine learning to study your voice pattern from past recordings and improve its response to your questions. You can delete these voice recordings, but in doing so you may degrade your user experience with Echo Plus.

Troubleshooting

Sometimes the Echo Plus does not listen to your voice or hangs carry out the following steps to get it back in action.

- Ensure that your device in not on MUTE. Check the LED ring in not RED. If it is RED, press the MUTE button again and start speaking.
- Ensure that Echo Plus is not receiving a software update.
- Unplug the device and leave it off for 60 sec and then plug it back again. It should mostly come back online by performing this action.
- If it still does not respond, leave it unplugged for a few hours and then plug it back again.
- Still Struggling? Try to reset your Echo Plus You will need to setup the device again so try to use this step sparingly. However, in most cases this does the trick.
- If the problem still persists, try to contact Amazon Customer Support.

Can't connect to the Bluetooth?

If you aren't able to connect your mobile device to the Amazon Echo Plus using Bluetooth the here are a few steps that you can follow.

Ensure that the device you are trying to connect is within 30 feet of the Amazon Echo.

The Bluetooth connection needs to be turned on.

Your mobile device needs to be paired with the Amazon Echo Plus and if it isn't paired you will need to say "Alexa pair".

From the Bluetooth settings on your mobile device select the options Amazon list so that it can connect to the device.

If you are still having trouble, then follow the following steps.

- Open the Alexa app and go to the Settings in it. Select the name of your Amazon Echo Plus from the options. This will clear all the devices that are currently paired.
- Unplug the power cord from the Amazon Echo Plus and then plug it back in after 30 seconds.
- Now retreat your mobile device again. Once the device is on you can turn the Bluetooth on from the settings menu.
- Say "(your wake word), pair". Amazon Echo Plus will respond with "ready to pair ". On your mobile device will need to open your setting menu and choose the option Echo-####
- You need to select the name of your Amazon Echo Plus from your mobile device. Amazon Echo Plus will respond with "connected with Bluetooth "if the connection was successful.

Echo Plus keeps disconnecting from my network?

This seems to be a common problem that a lot of Echo Plus users have been facing. Here are some things that you can try for solving this problem.

- You should reset your router: On your router, there should be a reset button, but the location of this can vary depending on the manufacturer and the model. If you can't find it, then proceed to the next step.

- Try rebooting your router: You will need to turn the router off and wait for 30 seconds before it back on. When you do this the Wifi services on the other devices will be interrupted. So, before you reboot the router you should probably ensure that no one is doing anything critical on his or her devices. So that they can save their work before the Wifi is turned off. If there's no improvement then move on to the next step.

- Reboot the router and let the Wifi be connected to only the Echo Plus and no other device: Yes, this indeed is a troublesome process. But it has proven to be effective. The Echo connects better when it is the first priority in the order of the Wifi connections. So, this means that you will need to disconnect all the other devices that are connected to the Wifi before you turn the Wifi on again. By doing this you will be able to ensure that the Echo Plus is going to get connected first. And once your Echo Plus is connected you can reconnect all the other devices. Proceed to the next step if this doesn't work.

- Get a backup power supply for your router: if you happen to reside in an area where there are brownouts or disruption in the electrical supply for a brief period of time, then you should consider getting a backup power supply for the router you are using. Even if the disruption was for a few seconds your entire Internet connection can be down. So, you will have to reset the main box. Still no luck? There is one last thing that you can try.

- Upgrade your router: if you are tech savvy, then you can fiddle with the settings of your router and try and optimize the connection to your Echo Plus. But it can be the case of having too many devices that are connected to the same router. Routers have a capacity to accommodate only a certain number of devices. Any additional device will cause excessive load on the router and it won't get connected. So, upgrading your router might be a good idea.

Echo isn't able to hear you clearly?

It can so happen that your Echo Plus might not be able to hear you clearly. Most often it is the problem with the location of the Echo. When the Echo is near any wall, the audio tends to bounce back. This causes a literal echo that can confuse the speech recognition ability of the Echo Plus. It could also be due to any interference from other electronic devices and this could cause the inability of the Echo Plus to recognize your commands. So, all you need to do is find a sweet spot for your Echo Plus so that it works better. The Echo Plus mobile app helps you not only record what the Echo Plus heard you say but it also gives you an option to let you decide whether or not Echo Plus heard you right. You can make use of this feature of deciding the best location for your Echo Plus.

Look around the room and think of a possible list of places where you can place the Echo, but the location chosen needs to be near an electrical outlet. You should also avoid all those places that have an uneven surface where the Echo Plus might get knocked over and also avoid those places where are any vents nearby including other sources of heat or cold. For each of the possible locations for the Echo Plus, you need to follow the instructions give here. You will need to plug the Echo Plus in the location that you desire and wait for it to say that it's ready. The place that you usually stand or sit at, say this to the Echo Plus "(wake word), your new location". For instance, you can say "Alexa: you are now on the coffee table".

If you are in the habit of interacting with your Echo Plus from different locations, try each of these in turn and add the different locations to the statement you are making. Like "Alexa: you are on the coffee table and I am in the foyer." Notice whether or not the light blue highlight that's present on the LED ring at the top the

Echo Plus is oriented towards your current location. This light is supposed to provide the indication of where the Echo Plus thinks you are. At times you will also get default error responses like, "I can't find the answer to the question I have heard", you needn't worry about this. Remember that you aren't trying to get a valid response from the Echo Plus. You can check the mobile Echo app to see whether or not the Echo Plus heard you properly.

When you are done with the above things then you should review the results of the placement test. By now you should have a good idea of the possible locations where the Echo Plus can hear you and these places are the typical places suited for your Echo Plus. So, all you need to do is move your Echo Plus to the new location you have decided on and you can enjoy much better conversations with Alexa.

Cannot discover a connected home device?

If Alexa isn't able to discover a smart home device then here are the steps that you can follow. The first thing that you will need to try would be:

- The home device you are trying to connect should be compatible with Alexa.
- You will need to link your third party account for devices that are connected to a hub, like Wink for instance.
- Check whether or not the device is set up properly in the companion app of the device. You can contact the manufacturer or visit their website if you aren't able to set up the device.
- Through the manufacturer's companion app you can update the software of your smart home device. These updates will help in improving the Wifi connection of the device.
- For discovering a smart home device on your Echo Plus, you will need to connect Alexa to the same Wifi network. For updating your Wifi in the Alexa app, you will need to go to

the settings, select the name of the device and click the option update Wifi.

- Personal Wifi networks are best suitable for Alexa and other smart home devices. Also, the Wifi devices at school or work might not allow unrecognized devices to connect to them.

How to delete your Voice Recordings

Delete Individual Recordings

- Open your Alexa app
- Tap Settings
- Tap History.
- Here, you will see a list of requests you have made since setting up your Echo.
- To delete a recording, tap it, and then tap Delete voice recordings.

Delete All the Recordings

- Head to Amazon
- Sign in and click Your Devices.
- Select Amazon Echo Plus,

Click *Manage Voice Recordings*

Conclusion

Hope this book has helped you make Amazon Echo Plus the center of your smart life and enabled you to organize your life seamlessly with Alexa at your command.

Continue on with your wonderful journey with the power of Amazon Echo Plus. Hope your doubts are removed and your life has eased. Since this is only the beginning, you will find more comfort and happiness with Alexa as you get more fluent with the device and the interface.

This is just the beginning, the Alexa rage is going to go global very soon and then you will see an explosion of Alexa Skills that will transform the way we live.

Wish you all the best automation possible in your life! Ah, Alexa! Come sit down.

Do You Want To Stay Updated With Alexa?

As discussed in the beginning of this book, please find the URL for the signup to our FREE weekly Alexa Newsletter. Each week we will send you NEW ways to use your Amazon Echo at Home, Work And Play.

http://www.amzecho.ontrapages.com/

The Amazon Echo and Alexa Enabled Devices are still in their infancy. In fact you are one of the EARLY ADOPTORS of this technology. The smart assistant industry is changing so fast with new devices, apps and skills being released almost every other day that it is almost impossible to STAY FRESH.

Staying in the know about new developments in the Smart Assistive Industry is what we are here for. Do not worry, we hate spam as much as you do and your details will be safe with us. Please go to http://www.amzecho.ontrapages.com/ to signup.

Did you like this Book?

Let everyone know by posting a review on Amazon. Just click here and it will take you directly to the review page.

And if want to learn some real DIY hack on your new Amazon Echo Plus do get in touch at help@dealhunteronline.com

Other Books You May Like

Appendix 1A

Amazon Alexa compatible products -

- Alottazs Labs Garageio (One Door)
- Amazon Dash Wand with Alexa (2017)
- Amazon Echo Look
- Amazon Echo Show (White)
- Aristotle by Nabi
- August Smart Lock
- August Smart Lock HomeKit Enabled (Dark Gray)
- smart driving assistant
- Belkin WeMo Dimmer Wi-Fi Light Switch
- Belkin WeMo Insight Switch
- Belkin WeMo Light Switch
- Belkin WeMo Mini Wi-Fi Smart Plug
- The nIFTTTy Belkin WeMo Switch + Motion
- Big Ass Fans Haiku Ceiling Fan with SenseME
- Big Ass Solutions Haiku L Series Ceiling Fan (Black)
- Big Ass Solutions Haiku Smart Ceiling Light (White Select)
- Bluemint Labs Bixi
- Brilliant Control
- C-Way Memoo
- Cambridge Sound Management Nightingale
- Carrier Cor 5C Thermostat
- Cnct IntelliPlug
- Ecobee3 Lite Smart Thermostat
- Ecobee3 Wi-Fi Smart Thermostat

- Ecobee4 Smart Thermostat
- Emerson Sensi Wi-Fi Programmable Thermostat
- Fabriq Alexa-Enabled Smart Speaker (Earl Grey)
- First Alert Onelink Environment Monitor
- Fitbit Charge 2 (plum/silver, large)
- Fremo Evo (Black)
- GE Cafe Series French door refrigerator with Keurig K-Cup Brewing System
- Fitbit Charge 2 Wireless Activity Tracker and Sleep Wristband (Large, Black/Silver)
- GE GTW860SPJMC
- GE Link Connected LED
- GE PHB920SJSS
- Geeni Energi
- GE Link Connected LED
- Halo Smart Labs Halo+ Smart Smoke & CO Alarm with Weather Alerts
- Hive Welcome Home Standard
- Honeywell Lyric T5
- iDevices Outdoor Switch
- Home8 Smart Garage Starter Kit
- Hubble Hugo
- Hydrao First
- iDevices Instant Switch
- iDevices Socket
- iDevices Switch
- iDevices Thermostat
- iDevices Wall Outlet
- iHome iSP8 SmartPlug
- Incipio CommandKit Wi-Fi Power Strip
- Incipio CommandKit Wi-Fi Switch
- Joule
- Leviton Decora Smart Wi-Fi Plug-In Dimmer
- LG Smart Instaview Door-in-Door Refrigerator (Black Stainless Steel)

- Lifx Color 1000 BR30 Wi-Fi LED Smart Bulb
- LG Hub Robot
- Oomi Home Starter Kit
- Orbit B-hyve (6 Station)
- Philips Hue Beyond Pendant Light Starter Kit
- Philips Hue Go
- Lifx Color 1000 Smart Bulb
- Lifx Plus Wi-Fi LED Smart Bulb
- Lifx White 900 BR30 Wi-Fi LED Smart Bulb
- Lucis Nubryte
- Lutron Caséta Wireless Lighting Starter Kit
- Neato Botvac Connected Robot Vacuum
- Nest Cam IQ Indoor Security Camera
- Nest Learning Thermostat Third Generation
- Onkyo VC-FLX1
- Ooma Telo
- Philips Hue White Ambiance
- Philips Hue White and Color Ambience Starter Kit A19
- Rachio Smart Sprinkler Controller Generation 2
- Ring Video Doorbell 2
- Samsung Powerbot VR7000
- Scout Home Security System (Arctic)
- Simplehuman Sensor Mirror Pro
- Simplehuman Wide-View Sensor Mirror
- Singlecue Gen 2
- SkyBell Video Doorbell
- Somfy One
- Switchmate Power
- TP-Link LB130 Multicolor Wi-Fi LED
- Ubtech Robotics Lynx
- Switchmate Bright

References

Amazon Echo Wikipedia

Amazon Alexa Skill Central

IFTTT Recipes

Love my echo

Echo Tricks

Echosim

Amazon.com

Made in the USA
San Bernardino, CA
12 December 2017